"She's Welcome to Her Disease"
Dementia Blog
[Volume Two]

Singing Horse Press 2013

"Situated near the middle of Susan M. Schultz's most recent
documentation of dementia is a wonderfully cryptic note: 'The
subject is forgetting but the writing is all memory.' *'She's Welcome
to Her Disease' [Dementia Blog, Volume Two]* is full of such astute
perceptions about the ambivalence we must face when con-
fronted with this disease. The book is the substantive result of a
compositional exploration that began in 2006 with *Dementia Blog*
and continued through six years of documenting her mother's
memoryless world to her death in June 2011. Schultz brings to
her sad and difficult project an impressive range of writing
abilities; she gestures through theatre, choreography, poetry,
medical, critical, and philosophical exposition, and yet manages
to shape this all into an accessible and engaging journal. It is a
poignant treatise on dementia written with grace and compas-
sion, as well as a story that honors death and dying with intel-
ligence and art."

—Fred Wah

"Susan M. Schultz accompanied her mother as she walked the
path from health to Alzheimer's, and from Alzheimer's to death.
In *'She's Welcome to her Disease' [Dementia Blog, Volume Two]*,
Schultz explores the wide range of experiences that families go
through in caring for loved ones with dementia. But rather than
a linear memoir, Schultz has crafted a volume of poetry,
essays, journal entries, observations, and even letters and e-mails
that mirror the lives of those of us on the Alzheimer's journey.
Schultz is a master explorer of language with a gift for composing
the lyrical, for targeting and naming an elusive emotion or nuance,
and for using words to create beauty and art from the mundane
and the devastating. An astute observer, she's attuned to the
poetry and art in the words and actions of the Alzheimer's
patients she witnesses. As artist and witness, Schultz incites not
only the visceral but the contemplative reaction, as well: Who,
in the end, has lost the ability to communicate—those of us who
are sick, or those of us who are whole? In the end, perhaps the
greatest gift Schultz gives us is the reminder that empathy and
compassion aren't solely found in the act of caring for another
human being. They also lie in the keen and respectful observance
of the human journey from birth to death."

—Beatriz Terrazas

"Susan M. Schultz's *'She's Welcome to Her Disease' [Dementia Blog, Volume Two]* has forced me to reconsider my negative relation to the blog, and in a more radical sense, to the memoir. *'She's Welcome to Her Disease'* is terribly intimate: carrying in cupped hands a memory, memory, and memories. A chronicle of events washing over a deeply feeling intelligence 'like jazz moving over the furniture' (as John Ashbery might have it)."

—John Emil Vincent

"'Anne of Manor Care Gables' meets *'Planet of the Apes* at Arden Courts'; Gertrude Stein's stanzas meet the dialogue of Alzheimer's patients; Roland Barthes' *Mourning Diary* meets Susan M. Schultz's *Dementia Blog*. Given that its subject is forgetting, there's an improbable plentitude of formal invention and wit in *'She's Welcome To Her Disease' [Dementia Blog, Volume Two]*, a comedy of the postmodern manner in which genres meet and mash up: now memoir, now essay, now play, now literary criticism, now documentary poem, the tropes of each genre always already borrowed by another. And though Schultz means to point out that the postmodern manner is eerily well suited to the linguistic world of the dementia patient, Arden Courts is a world in which parataxis, aphasia, and non sequitur signify neither aesthetic play nor critical acumen but neurological disorder and an irreversible loss of memory. So what meaning survives when all the words have switched hats forever? Schultz's sustained witnessing and graceful acceptance of her mother's death provide 'A mode of art that is not power, but offers us a model' of compassionate ethics, playful intelligence, and powerful memorial. It is hard to imagine a more loving tribute to a life."

—Brian Teare

Cover design and art: Gaye Chan.

ISBN 978-0-935162-51-6
Singing Horse Press
5251 Quaker Hill Lane
San Diego, CA 92130

Singing Horse Press titles are available from the publisher at
singinghorsepress.com or from Small Press Distribution (800)
869-7553, or at www.spdbooks.org.

"She's Welcome to Her Disease"
Dementia Blog
[Volume Two]

Susan M. Schultz

—Martha J. Schultz

(October 25, 1917—June 14, 2011)

Table of Contents

Anne of Manor Care Gables

The residents are all relinquished.

The residents, who had birthed or adopted us, are left at the stoop of assisted living with a suitcase and some photographs.

The residents, who had wanted us (we hope), are always the wrong age, the wrong gender, always wear their clothes in the wrong way.

The residents enter their asylum wanting ice cream. For a time they want to go home, but cannot remember how to get to the street whose name escapes them, or the city they never lived in but whose name they know.

The residents do not recognize themselves, all boxed up and memorialized beside their doors.

The residents all have the same hair style: Founding Fathers for the women, and 9 to 5 for the men.

The residents live in a geography of wings, of corridors, of rooms, of chairs.

The residents use magical thinking to unmagical results. They emerge from the closets under their children's staircases, clutching dolls or pencils or purses.

The residents know that you are stealing from them, and you and you. You are taking their keys, their money, their clothes, their words.

The residents do not know why she fell and hit her head and left blood on the carpet. It might have something to do with John's children, or with her being in the wrong room, or with a grudge that no one can possibly remember.

The residents do not know why they live in a parking lot, why no one comes to drive them home.

The residents are not as terrified of themselves as you are of them.

The residents are like children. No one says that children are like them.

The residents include a president, a film director, a chef, an artist, and a boxer. Or so we tell them.

The residents cannot know the plot devices that will lead them to find a new family or to work on the farm or to dye their hair green.

The residents do not understand PR. They do not know to say they live in a home run by the Champions of Care, 1999.

Waiting Adults

Martha (92) has a sweet temper, though sometimes she says
"no," pushes her caregivers away. She speaks only when spoken
to, consumes a can of Ensure each day through a bendy straw,
and walks only with the assistance of others. She does not inter-
act with peers, but sits slumped over in a chair. Will not submit
easily to bathing or having her hair done.

Florence (90) has a lovely face that features deep folds under
blue eyes. She wears dapper sweaters and talks constantly,
though her sentences never end as they promise to begin. Took
care of a sister until her sister died. A curious woman, she
occasionally rifles through the possessions of visitors. Speaks
with a strong New England accent.

Joe (85) is well dressed and sports a mustache. He moves
constantly, as if he has somewhere to go. He may have been
the drummer in a band. Victim of family expectations, he takes
unkind words to heart and must be reassured by another adult
before he calms down.

Ed (82) has been on our waiting list for nine years now. He has
his wits about him (a very good long-term memory, decent
short-term); aside from inappropriate sexual remarks, he is kind
and appreciates his foster situation. Ed was an engineer, and
talks a blue streak about the Baby Bells.

Joseph (78) is mostly taciturn, but becomes a good old boy at
dusk, glad handing his friends and caregivers, revealing the soul
of a salesman. He has some delays in his movements, but can
still walk on his own and does not yet suffer incontinence.

Sylvia (90) wants a job. She worked as a seamstress and owned
a shop. She also dreams of traveling to Europe and back to
New York City, where she grew up. Sylvia is conspiratorial, and
knows who's been messing with whom. She wears dresses and
high black socks, carries a black purse and a newspaper with her.

Pat (82) is sweet and kind and listens to Christian radio. She
misses her baby, and often cries over him. Aside from her nearly
constant depression, manifested in frequent sobbing, Pat is
a good friend to her peers, and they to her. Her memory box
shows a heavy set woman with a wide smile.

Jan (76) appears stoic, but mutters, and occasionally gets angry.
Does not appear to have family that visits her, though there are
photographs in her box of a husband and adopted daughter.
Carries a worry line in her forehead, but is in good health, aside
from mental deficits.

Ann (82) is a very proper woman. She wears skirts and slacks
and carries a purse. She gossips a great deal, and is overly in-
terested in her peers' activities. Has been seen walking the halls
with the new man, a former school principal with a Roman nose.
Suffers occasional outbursts of profanity, but is never loud.
Hospitable, she invites you into her room.

Estella (85) is kind only if you speak to her in Spanish. She does
not like cheese, nor does she like it when her bag is missing from
her walker. Glowers at company, but eats a good sized portion of
her meals, and especially enjoys red juice.

Jenny (86) has a raggedy Ann that she hugs constantly and
whose feet she sucks. She often talks to herself about pleasure;
there is some inappropriateness to her conversation. She loves
Pat, and offers her the doll when she sees her. Jean still talks, but
her conversation is rambling, often incoherent. We are told that
she may have suffered a head injury.

Janice (84) was born in Shanghai and translated Japanese docu-
ments for the State Department. If you tell her to use a fork, she
will put it in her right hand and then eat with her left. She cannot
speak, but communicates with her eyes and her hands. Often
appears surprised. Looks neat in a buzz cut.

News

Little **Sylvia** (87) found a new placement two months ago. A pert
woman with New York accent, she sang through lunch and supper,
laughed loudly at her own jokes.

P has died. She was the light haired woman with glasses and a walker. Name forgotten.

Reader's Report

I sat in a wooden rocking chair reading. A woman who sucks the
gums behind her sunken cheeks and walks at a forward angle
put first one worn hand, then the other, on the arms of my chair.
She stared at me, chin to chin, muttered a few words I did not
catch. I looked down at section 10 of Chad Sweeney's *An
Architecture:*

the nouns are verbs
conduit between *I* and *I*

from which the fish the fowl--
looking

into it
a face

breaks on the well water
source and structure

--the double

helix
a thrush's voice

of the body and be
yond the body

is the meaning of our talk

and then later:

art is

the ghost between us

Another woman, older than my mother but not by much,
admired my blue Obama 44 bag, wondered if I had to go to
school to learn how to make it. Tempted to say I went to school

so as *not* to know how to make it, I watched her as she carefully examined the bag.

This last woman talks a lot--about her sister Charlotte, about bags, about the knocking on a door she thinks is for her--but the momentum of talk trips her up. She runs out of words, falls silent, begins another story.

I noted to a Chinese woman that she has grandchildren. She smiled, turned her attention to her neighbor's rice, which had spilled off her plate. Her neighbor moved grains of rice to the place mat on the other side of the plate. Grain by grain.

My mother rests quietly all day, recovering from pneumonia. While others nap in their chairs, she sits awake. Occasionally she smiles, or looks unhappy when someone talks about her. "They really should shave her chin," says a volunteer, as my mother visibly ignores her.

--Tuesday, February 17, 2009

My name, which does not belong to me: Olivia Rosenthal, Paul Valéry, and Dr. Alzheimer

Olivia Rosenthal's *On n'est pas là pour disparaître*, was published by Éditions Gallimard in 2007. It is what might be called a documentary novel about Alzheimer and his disease, in voices that range from that of Monsieur T, who has Alzheimer's and dreams of America; his wife, whom M. T. stabbed; their daughter, toward whom the father has made sexual advances; and the author's (is it?), who meditates on writing about a disease she hopes not to acquire. She, who does not have children, also contemplates what it might mean to be a descendant of Dr. Alzheimer, given his name, a blood-line's memory of the disease that denotes memory's extinction. It's a busy book, but one that can be turned (metaphorically) to many angles, like a sad diamond. Then there are dialogues like this one:

Combien avez-vous d'enfants? [How many children do you have?]
Plusieurs. [Several]
Pouvez-vous dire leurs noms? [Can you say their names?]
Oui, bien sûr, ce n'est pas de leur faute. [Yes, of course, it's not their fault.]

Such are dementia's non sequiturs.

———————

This was the week my introductory level students wrote documentary poems about a relative they do not know well. One women wrote hers on the backs of photographs of her grandmother, doctored ones (as it were). Her grandmother suffers from Alzheimer's. One photograph shows her grandmother's face, cupped inside two hands. Monsieur T. stabbed his wife; we can't condemn him because he doesn't have the wherewithal to act as an Alzheimer's sufferer; he is one. Demented people cannot act.

———————

"Each moment exists at the center of an incalculable confluence
of things. Some of these factors we have singled out and called
by different names (sociological factors, political, psychological,
spiritual, etc.) but some remain nameless. In the same way that
physicists have not yet determined all the components that
make up matter, we do not completely know what creates and
makes up 'the moment.' What we do know is that the moment
has a texture, and that in memory it can also be experienced as a
weight--can press against the flesh." (Ellen Hinsey, letter to Uta
Gosmann)

____

And yet among the heaviest moments are those spent with
Alzheimer's patients, those whose memories are lightest, have
flown, whose bodies seem to have supplanted their memories,
like containers that take the place of what they contained. The
textures of forgetting are dense, heavier than the furniture in the
"home," the solid entertainment centers and Ethan Allen chairs,
the suburban couches. Forgetting occurs (can it occur, really?) in
comfort. But it's stubborn, immovable.

____

Rosenthal asks us to perform exercises. One is to calculate the
number of persons to whom you refer in the past tense, but who
are still alive. (And those to whom we refer in the present who
have died?) My advice to a student was to ask her to "change the
eternal present--experiment with other tenses." Dementia offers
us the conditional, the provisional tense, the not-present or not-
past or not-future tense. Invent a new tense for those who have
forgotten you. It changes you, to be forgotten so.

____

It becomes harder to believe in memory once you've seen some-
one lose it. Paul Valéry writes of "Memory heaping and building
in the dusk of our souls holds itself ever ready to restore to us
what the universal flux withdraws from us instant by instant." Is
that like the restoration of an old house? Or like the restoration of
a monarchy? Those restorations are not to what was. I had friends
in Williamsburg, Virginia who thought they lived in a restored

colonial house, but actually inhabited a reproduction. Who could not say they had the better plumbing, the stronger walls? Better than memory is a new construction like that. Reproduction in the age of.

———————

It's hard to believe that we are other than our memories when we see someone lose hers. She is alive, her voice (which is also crucial to our sense of her) remains much the same. But her voice has lost its words, except a very few. It is memory that furnishes Crusoe's island, according to Valéry, "malleable memory, pliable to the moment's needs." But her island is her voice, and its shorelines have been eroded and eroded more. She says little beyond how nice it is to hear that everything is ok. To what part of her is that a solace? Perhaps some memory of her worries, those that fueled her before she forgot how to fret.

———————

Rosenthal devotes nearly a chapter to the names of diseases named after people, diseases you/she/I do not want to die of. The names are markers of anxiety; simply to call them out is to raise one's blood pressure, begin to imagine end games, pains, self-losses. There is violence at moments of recognition that one is related to Dr. Alzheimer by brain tissue, by forgetting. Monsieur T. tried to kill his wife. My mother attacked a caregiver. This (or that) is the moment when all agency is taken away. The name, violence, and then "home." We care give, we assist live, we take care of them. You can see memory, like a dream of violence, draining from their eyes.

———————

Quel est votre prénom? [What is your name?]
Il ne m'appartient pas. [It does not belong to me.]

--Sunday, September 20, 2009

Note: Uta Gosmann, "Spacing the Past: The Mnemotechniques of Ellen Hinsey." *Common Knowledge* (14:2) Spring, 2008: 283.

--She sits slumped over to her right in a chair in the Country Lane common area. "Sit up, Martha," Christine and I tell her. She props her left elbow on the armrest for a few moments, then slumps over again. Christine wanted her hair done before I came; it's short, plastered oddly to her head. She wears black sneakers with pink lace holders, white socks, black slacks, shirt and brown suede jacket. When she stands up to go into the next room for lunch, she looks smaller than before, needs guidance to walk the several paces to sit next to Sylvia, the woman who speaks loudly, sings in the hall. One of the workmen awakened her, flapping his arms, pretend-flying.

--I'm so tired at lunch (lost sleep, jetlag, a trip to mom's lawyer and tax preparer in Arlington) that I excuse myself, lie down on mom's bed and go to sleep. She's in room 9, has a new neighbor since last year. Christine brings mom in after lunch to go to the bathroom, then leaves. Then I hear loud noises. "YOU'RE TRY- ING TO KILL ME, I KNOW YOU'RE TRYING TO KILL ME!!!!" When I go to the common room, I see the fake Christmas tree's been knocked over. The glass angel damaged again, its wing broken. Light strings in knots. Christine takes the tree down. It was Pat, whom I remember as a placid woman last February. She's angry now, back in her room, banging on the door.

--Later in the afternoon, Pat comes out; Christine gets her to sit in the common room, brings her Ensure in a small cup. Pat is nearly past language. Lifts arms up, as if to place them on the handle bars of a motorcycle, says, NNNNNNNNNNNO, NNNNNNNNNNO. Begins a sentence one way, finishes it, or fails to finish it, another. Joe, the man she shoved, does the same. "Julie," he says, nothing more. Pat's eyes get big when she gets mad, and she's mad now. She comes over to me to ask, "what can I do for you?" Can't finish her question. "What do you think you could do for me?" I ask. She holds her shirt up at the bottom. Christine intervenes; leads her to a chair.

--Joe says he has a "hole." He keeps telling me about falling out of bed, waiting for three hours, crying out, and getting this hole, larger than a quarter that he shows me with his hand. He has a cut on his forehead. But the hole is on his leg. Christine raises up his pant leg. "You have an abrasion," she says. I try to help by reducing the word to "scrape."

--Of my mother, Lena says to those in the common room, "She used to be my best, first customer in the mornings." Lena holds a large white ball, which she tosses back and forth while she talks. "Now it's you," she tells a woman in the first row.

--My mother dozes as the television runs. Before lunch it's *Young Frankenstein*. We saw that movie together. Now five old people sit and sleep while Gene Wilder vamps. After lunch, *Planet of the Apes* movies come on. Charlton Heston sweet talks a young woman, thin and breasty, who doesn't speak. "Can you talk? Talk?" he demands. There is hair on his chest, loud teeth in his mouth. He gives her his dog tag. Says "Taylor" and points to himself. Says the name again, again points. Disappears, with a gun, on his horse into thin air. The second one, the one who looks like Heston, has the woman, who still can't speak English, take him to the ape village. A military ape rants about war, invasions, the need to conquer. A female ape mutters against the war. The male ape wins. Heston's clone is captured, escapes. I lose track, wander off. Mom still dozes.

--Something has changed for me. This visit is easier than before. I am used to seeing my mother like this. She doesn't talk, smiles only occasionally, stares at the TV or into space, slumps over, sleeps a bit. I wonder why it feels easier now. Why there's less need to lock in, hold everything in memory until later in the motel room, though I do. I try to remember which residents are gone. There was the woman with the dolls around her neck; the woman who carried a kleenex box wherever she went; the woman who seemed European. Others I do remember: the grandmother who could not remember how many grandkids she had. Dr. French still has a room, memory box. A Rev. B wanders the halls, as if to minister to the residents. It takes time to realize he is one.

--Amber who works the front desk, still hasn't sent me inauguration photos. She recommends a Vienna restaurant, Maple Ave, where I go for dinner. Beef stew. Reminds me of home.

--Wednesday, January 6, 2010

The Science of Happiness

--Science shows that people get happier as they age. One woman, now 87, plays the piano, attends classes, can be seen in photos with friends at lunch. PBS tells us that we are more calm when we're older; double so at 40 than at 20. We know our character strengths; we practice them. People are more resilient than you might think. The juvenile delinquent is a thoracic surgeon; the woman with cancer meditates now, changes wigs with less frequency. Positive psychology works for soldiers in the field.

--At the caregiver agency there are stacks of boxes, at least four of them, one on top of the other. They are full of cigars. The man is 90 and has plenty of money, so he orders cigars. Every so often they have to clear them out. "I keep thinking I started as a public health nurse," says the boss. Now she ships cigars to soldiers in Afghanistan, Iraq. They'll be used, says a woman whose niece is over there now. His company could probably use some.

--It's a war movie today; men in helmets sit in mud. War movie music, oddly sweet, so it's an old movie. "Her daughter, he loved her."

--One of the two Sylvia's breaks the lunch time silence. "It's so quiet in here, it's scary," she says, loudly. Like the other Sylvia, she's from New York. "Where in New York?" Christine asks, breaking her own silence as she spoons the goulash-y dish onto the plates. "The best place in New York!" Turns out it's the Bronx, so I say the Yankees won the World Series this year. "Yes, that's why I love them," she says, "but unfortunately, I didn't know." I'm helping my mother eat, fork full by fork full; she no longer eats willingly, when Sylvia starts giving me the A-OK hand gesture. "Awl daughtas should be lwike that!" Yesterday she was on the arms of a daughter-in-law and grandson, fresh from the cold air. Today she wears a brown and black dress and black knee socks.

--Joe is eating his lunch by the back window, facing another man but not looking at him. A man and a woman come and stand behind and beside him; his daughter and son-in-law.

"You spilled food on your pants! There's food everywhere! And how about your leg? Did you cut it? My husband is just out of surgery," she says, jangling her keys. He holds up his bandaged arm. "Did you know about that? He had surgery! Hasn't had breakfast yet, so we gotta go." Gone.

--A few minutes later, Christine says to Joe, "no don't even think that; you weren't mean to them, you were having your lunch. Get it out of your head."

--Mom goes to the beauty shop. Under the dryer sits Pat; yesterday, she tore down the Christmas tree on Country Lane. Today, Pat is weeping. Emma tries to console her but fails. Pat weeps because of a baby. She utters other parts of words, sounds, but the one word that works is "baby." Then she begins to speak with a strong voice; she had four children and they had books and. The voice scrambles again. We arrive at the moment when language slams shut.

--Florence talks all the time to herself when she's not napping. Doe-eyed, she wears a thick colorful sweater. She talks about Massachusetts, New Bedford. She says she does not have a good musical voice. She says she'll sing, but her voice. Christine tells me that Florence and her sister took care of each other until the sister died. "The MacKenzies, I said The MacKenzies!"

--At the common room, where mom hardly ever goes any more, Ed, the man who courts the ladies, wishes he could give Martha chocolate (against the rules), says New York was great except for the Irish section. Smell of pee in the corners. Mary Lou (a caregiver) says it was the Germans. Michael is gone, who led the discussions, replaced by a young man who remembers deli sandwiches in Brooklyn for $2 or $3. Mary Lou pitches in about pickles on the plate.

--The flowers. I'm known for the flowers I send from Hawai'i. They keep the place cool when the flowers arrive.

--Esther says not everyone realizes, but the residents take care of her, too. The way they talk to her, she knows what we go through.

--At the hair dresser, I ask mom if she remembers me. "I remember you," she says, and smiles. In the common area, Betty from India asks mom if she remembers her daughter. "No, that's not my daughter," she says, and smiles.

--The email header is "um," from a poetry friend who wonders how I'm feeling better about it all this time. This is not cruel distance, nor is it enlightened detachment. "Whatever you do, that's your 'real' life," my mom would say.

--I punch in 6s and 3s and 1s. I keep getting them wrong. The door won't open. A resident is walking toward the door, feeling the molding on the wall as he goes. Door clicks. I open it, and he says something about going out. I push the door closed against his voice.

--Thursday, January 7, 2010

Sundowning

--Sundown. An orange circle filled in behind Arden Courts. Inside, Sylvia, who gives me the a-ok at lunchtime, demands $2. "I just wanna get home; it's close by." She's a businesswoman, has a house—two house! She's in knee socks again, a dress, waves around a brown wallet. Someone picked her pocket, left her with nothing. "Does anyone know me well enough to lend me two dollahs?" she demands. "Who's in charge here? Where's the office? $2 charity!" The office is down the hall and to the right, Betty says, although it's down the hall, through a locked door and to the left. Even so, Sylvia comes back with the boss, who says her son is coming later. "Does anyone know me enough to give me $2!" Then, somehow, she has a dollar. Her refrain changes, in number only. One dollah; her Bronx accent thickens. "Everyone's a liah! It's not funny!" She's not a charity case, you know.

--Her son and grandson are signing in as I leave. Just so you know, the boss tells them. Her clothes are on her bed and she's ready to go.

--I wonder why I feel better this time. I wonder why I do not. I wonder if my reader still feels what I feel, or if we now diverge like paths at Arden Courts, those that never go anywhere except around and back to where they began. I wonder if the text's immediacy wears down, wears out, wears away. If bereavement ends with acceptance, even before death comes down Country Lane, high stepping past the piglet at the entrance and the tiny clothes hanging on a line and past the suburban furnishings and the large television, past the generic old-time photos to room 9, where Martha Schultz lives behind her name.

--Oprah interviews a woman whose surgeon husband was a thief and a cheat. "Believe what people tell you about themselves the first time they say it," Oprah quotes Angelou. And when was the first indication he was not who he seemed to be? (It had something to do with his shoes and the time of day.)

--Mom responds to photos when wifi kicks in, late afternoon. Facebook photos of the cat, the dogs ("cute dog!"), the girl, the boy, the husband, the President (he's the one after Bush, mom, a better one), some birds of paradise. She laughs, even. Not a laughter of recognition but.

--Pat is happy today. She still talks about children, still begins with words that dissolve into stuttered syllables. Another woman addresses me; I don't realize she's speaking Dutch, I only know I do not understand. Ann, who carries her purse everywhere, confides in me that "they tried to bullshit me" and "you know where they stick things," before inviting me into her room. I stay outside.

--Did Pat suffer yesterday when she wept, or the day before, when she pulled the tree down? Does Pat know she feels better now, coming just a little too close to me, to L, but not to bully us, as she does Joe? (None of us remember duration well, the newspaper tells us, but we remember events rather than years, months, days.) If there is no event to remember, or memory to record event, has there been suffering, joy, astonishment? The correct answer is yes. I think. Fill in the dot.

--L tells Pat she loves her, and Pat says more about the kids. Her eyes are dark moons, her hands white as if cold, her voice velvety, even when her anger starts. The common area is full, well-dressed residents in their formal chairs, half awake, the other half slumped over. One man wears a tie; Joe wears one new white tennis shoe and one white sock; Ed burps loudly; my mother sits quietly in her rocker. She says she's happy I came.

--Friday, January 8, 2010

World Cup

Pat (78) rises from her chair—a one, a two, a one two three—
stands as if hanging from invisible wire—spins slightly, on the
verge--left foot--forward—totters--catches "self"—turns—in slow
weave—sends right foot out—in pink sock--into open territory
with slip-on canvas shoe—pirouettes on common room floor—
war movie music backg . . .—slowly—eyes not on feet—nor on
the near distance--wavers, stalls, re-starts—hangs—her body
does not move so fast—large & yet precarious in air—feet stutter
toward Joe's chair—Joe (76) clutches her doll—one foot clips J's
leg—outstretched--the fall begins—slowly from foot & head—no
contact between—her body's mass gathering toward—one knee
& the next—elbows—[fall sounds]—spectator B (77) groans, rises
from his chair--Pat sobs—doll collapsed on floor—body flung
outward--hand outstretched—volitional—

Assumptions

--Some residents of Arden Courts destroy their memory boxes,
rip out the photos of themselves. Hence the box with fluffy dogs
in it; another box contains only parts of old photographs, air-
planes from the Air & Space Museum, tiny grandchildren gazing
up. Oblique boxes. "This is my room," Ann says to me, pointing at
her box, its old photograph of her. Does the box remind her of her
past, or only of her door, located next to it? Direction divorced
from history. Walmart plans to build a box store next to The
Wilderness battlefield. Each of its shelves will be a monument to
forgetting, its tenor and its vehicle.

--"I assumed she was always quiet, polite," the caregivers tell
me. I say she told funny stories, loved to talk. I recognize the
looks in their faces. This is who she is, has always been. This is
who she is now, because I remember her this way. Her loss of my
memory is my memory of her, long enough that she has become
the woman in the rocking chair, not the woman of her stories.

--My neighbor to LA was in his 20s, wore an NFL jacket, a Dodgers
cap, had a thin goatee and spoke into his cell phone in Spanish. I
asked if he liked the Dodgers. He asked what I thought of the
Redskins' coach. I said I didn't know. He talked about the
Wizards, the Caps, the Raiders, the Cowboys. Then: his
grandmother dropped dead at 50 in front of the television in
El Salvador. She thought too much; it killed her. (He made a
signal with his hand of a mind churning.) Half her family killed
by rebels, husband, children, grandparents. Her daughter, his
mother, age 47, multiple surgeries. She wants to build a house
in Salvador and live there by herself. "Crazy idea," he tells me,
told her. He fixed air conditioners for a while, worked in res-
taurants, pubs, had his Cowboy's shirt stolen by Redskins fans.
Wife in L.A., he wants to move back. Her dog died of cancer and
she couldn't let go. She wanted to be alone after the dog died.
"That's what I don't like about pets," he says. "They die."

--Sunday, January 10, 2010

Mom Report

Susan,

I am due to see your mom tomorrow. The staff at Arden Courts
got in touch with me to discuss possibly getting a hospice
consultation for your mom. Hospice is not only for when people
are actively dying and can offer a lot of additional support and
supervision for clients. Your mom is still the same at this time,
no real change. They thought it would be nice for her to have
the additional support. She eats fair and is not that involved or
interested in activities anymore. Her weight is stable though. My
thoughts are, she may not qualify at this time, but I wanted to
get your thoughts on having them do a consultation.

[J]

I reread the email for the phrase "Hospice is not only for when
people are actively dying." "Actively dying." I know what it
means, but I want to parse it. Is her dying then passive? Is that
what dementia is, an inactive verb for dying?

There has been such a slowness to her passing. It can hardly be
called "passing," this way station on the way to not being in
her chair, not not seeing what is before her, save a few photos to
make her smile (a dog, a cat, a child).

--Tuesday, April 13, 2010

Memorial Day at the Alzheimer's Home

[on television around the corner from the lunch room: *The Devil's Brigade*]

The speaker of most lines is an old woman with a New England accent. There is music in the background.

"I want to see my two younger rooms."

"You wouldn't expect her to pick your feet, would you?"

"Everyone has feelings."

"Just forget it!"

"My place--there--they didn't give you--gauze--because she didn't really want to do it--maybe it was her daughter--which would be who--give it all back to her and . . . house, yeah, had it described, especially."

"I think legally they can't do that."

Pat enters on the arm of a social worker. Pat's face is blue, her shirt is blue. Pat still moans, though more quietly than last time. The swelling's gone down, I'm told. Are you upset about something? the social worker asks her, after they sit at the window. "Every boy that you are."

Don't eat the ice. She eats the ice. Moves a cube from one plastic glass to another, her fingernails pink, like mom's. Her neighbor who doesn't speak indicates there's something wrong. She pushes back the table cloth, lifts her glass, tries to place it in her neighbor's bowl of pear slices.

"Candy. We've been a single and a diamond. Have to get a new job. A sensitive person. They have squares and they have one place to another."

Children. Children who need other children. And yet letting our grown up pride. Like children.

"That jacket, 12, try to change, 18 is it?"

People who need people are the luckiest people in the world. One very special person, your soul, half and now you're whole, the luckiest people in the world.

"Look over that car talking."

"NO CHEESE!"

I'm in love again and the feelings. Yes. And I know what to do.

"Pay for it--cash.
Another one she did. I know she made she seemed to travel 7.
Yes she said, just the one."

My love went to London, left not returned, I'm going to London.

"The first guy. After I, you were, yes I was surprised.
Avoid 5.
1, 2, and then oy 5.
They get I don't"

*There's a story told
To love easy to learn women promise
She never sighed or cried.*

"Think so I put that on before I finished it
Her engine and I think it's moving" (regards sweet potato from above, below).

*Every rolling stone
Home sweet home
I'm a rolling stone until today*

"That's what it was they, they told her
We did we saw it
8 books 8 hours the time we spent.
They were forced to visit

50 of age."

Railroad track
Taken on back
Why did I decide to go?

Mrs. Lee is Chinese, translated for the State Department. Speaks no language now. Her son, a doctor, comes on the weekends, but not this one.

WHY DO I ALWAYS GET THE SMALL PART?

"Sadie's pastor.
Werner's yeah."

ICE CREAM!!

God bless the child that's got his own.

"I haven't got a pan.
If I can get in 6 towns.
By color except by or black
I know she think she had her
(laughs) came up & says"

Something's bound to begin

I remember
My mother was at Anzio.

--Monday, May 31, 2010

NO CHEESE

[Monday. Common area: television, on. Music in background.]

Act One: 10 a.m.

My mommy's having a baby! A baby, a baby, a baby!

Gloria and Pat sit on the sofa.
Pat's eyes dark, deep, her face white as powder.
Gloria has her head on Pat's right shoulder.

Look! Two babies. Twins! The babies, the babies, the babies!

"I can't hear a word you're saying."

"I said get out!"

"It's hard for her because she dddddd." [Hands flutter at waist]

Pat tries to stand up.
Gloria tries to kiss her right arm.
Pat falls back.
They resume their position.

*A vicious German defense brought the Allied advance to a halt at
Casino. People say I look 10 years younger; I look 10 years younger.*

"Do you remember World War II, mom?"
"No."

Pat begins to cry. She embraces K, who starts to take her for a
walk.

"Where are your shoes? You need shoes to walk. You need to
stop crying or we can't go for a walk."
Pat and Gloria resume positions on the couch.

*I've been looking for a long time for someone to talk to and you're it
because you can't understand one word I say to you. I want to talk
about my girl back home. You I can tell the truth to*

s s s s s s s - v v v v v v v - s s s s
guh guh gonna go
There wasn't much time to think about women

Pat is cold, she's cold. She crosses her arms over pink and white
striped blouse and a pink cross on a pink necklace. She wipes her
cheeks on the bottom of her shirt.

"Marvelous! Good. Nothing." This woman, also in stripes, runs
off with my mother's elbow straw from her can of Ensure. "How
do you do your air?"

The luckiest people in the world

Act II: 4:30 p.m.

"Yer not talkin to yerself--I'm listenin'." [Florence to self]

*Why oh why can't I
They love everyone but you on top of this f__ hill.*

"She's a witch, I tell ya--that's what she is."

"Are you with the police again? Your mother asks me out for
beers, but I think I'm too young for her. We had a luau the other
day, the hula dancers had their tops on, very disappointing.
When you go back to Hawai'i, send me a shrunken head, ok, but
make sure the eyes are closed."

Florence: "He showed us that, I was wanting to go to the 5th
floor; didn't know how to, must be the 1st floor where they cook
stuff."

"They don't care about us."
"What's your first name?" Susan

"What's your name?" Susan

"Susan, and I still don't know it."

tangerine -- [gunfire] -- across the pond, yes she has

"Ruth, what is your name?"

"I'm Martha's daughter."
"I guess not."

"I'm going to do half a bugle,
Shiloh fast--
Is she going to win you, too?
But they'll be all right.
What we're going to do and have Ann's lot."

"I'D KICK HER ASS."

"They're all happy on this side
I got enough enough
Disquella, disk-la
That's the porty of the way."

"NO CHEESE!!!!"

"The name of the name of someone who is very cloned?
How is your doing?"

Mom: "don't bother me, don't bother me."

"Is your mom and dad doing it?"

"I'll make a noise."

J weeps over dinner. Her neighbor says:
"You're one of my favorite people."

"I lost my keys."
"That was peas, too."
"4 5 5 5 5 5
Her story is see you in a better place."

"You're the classiest gal in the whole world.
Don't be frightened."

Maybe this time I'll

"I want to go to the police
yes yes yes
to do something."

"Please don't throw us out.
Don't shut us off, please."

"I want to GET OUT,
what they're doing to me
NO NO."

ACT III: After dinner

"Have you heard the one about the mushrooms?"

"Have you heard the one about the two carrots?"

--Tuesday, June 1, 2010

"She's Welcome to Her Disease"

Stanzas in Meditation I

[Television on. Background music.]

WATSH! WATSH! Where's my watsh?

Mom pushes the inhaler away.
Mom pushes the Ensure away.
Mom sits next to Pat, without the loving lean of Pat and Gloria,
yesterday.

P: "I'm fine. I'll wawawa dyu unnnnnn." She starts to cry.

"That makes me happy because lulu. Lulu, yes
I hope it's my father where it's cuz you kids don't have to be like
that.
My back hurts: a little old lady that's me.
You wad it you dad it you got it you dat.
These are beautiful things.
I think it's perfect good,
if that's what we're getting it at [$5 off].
Turn him around you could get them back
because we need them; she wanted to was
helping fine with us help us, you don't have
too much it'll come.
I see it's over dere dere or not,
I just don't have a rose
because I might break it.
You done good
Your station but you're good
were nice were; I bet she's
welcome to her disease.
$5 off $25; where I going?"

"She's wagging in her tail
and she was feeling bad."

Gloria sucks on the black cloth foot of her doll with striped
socks.

"DON'T PUT ANYTHING IN THE SOAP!"

Gloria chews on doll's foot.
"I'll lie down and this is so good this is so good
& bound to feel that way."

Pat: "W Y NNN
H I I I I I I I I I
n n n n n n n n n
a a a a a a a a a a" [sound up, sound down]

Gloria: "It's one lake that came out."

J: "This lady is a good lady, can't pretend.
Things have to be good. All ready for good people."
[Walks around the room, pats everyone on the arm.]

Pat: H H H H H A A H A A A A

Gloria: "I have to take this table and shout!
We can read now!" [drops doll by dress to floor, falls asleep]

LIST OF CASUALTIES

dead
dead
dead
amputated
dead

N: "Barbie Barbie / Barbie Barbie / Barbie Barbie / (goes into
the dining room) /
Barbie Barbie / Barbie Barbie / Barbie Barbie / etc."

Pat gets up, shuffles, does a slow circular dance, trips on G's
shoe, falls.

Stanzas in Meditation II

Dinner time. Only Martha refuses to move to the dining room.
She watches Leonardo di Caprio promise the Irish vote to the
Sheriff. She will not move.

She will not move for B.
She will not move for Susan.
She will not move for the young African man.
She will not move for R.
She will not move for E.
She will not move for Susan.

Susan and Martha sit in the television room.
Martha wants her to go away.
Martha waves her arm when anyone comes near.
Leave Martha alone.
She will come later or she will not come at all.

R tells E to tell Susan to leave the room.
It's Susan's visit. She's never this angry. She always comes, if not
at first, then the second time you reach out for her hands.

B gets her into the dining room.
You can come back now.

Stanzas In Meditation III

Gloria: "If you can go home, then grant it is!"

Steve comes to see his mother.
"You open da stoah?"
He doesn't have a store.
"You didn't open da stoah?"

Florence: "Not long, but over 7.
What do they put outside.
When people asked information,
They'd know it in opposition.

And that might we put on the was
a cover, he liked doing it too.
A bit from the door, so people
could cast away, he's resting him
causing him if he got ready.
He had one of the other
give a test one of the girls--
he dropped her on the floor
and it was me.

It's ok. The only time I talked to him.

Not against but sort of
they were having a good time
a nice church, he pays attention"

Gloria: "Under my rough.
If you give her Laos, invilleagable."

Stanzas In Meditation IV

A scream.
J has fallen.
"Get up!"

"Oh G O D [screams]"
Her head is bleeding.
"Oh God I'm dead.
I don't want to go.
Oh I'm DEAD.
Oh God please help me."

"It's too late now."

"SCUM!
Get off my god damn"

Pat: "againagainagainagainagainagain."

Sylvia: "She didn't fall.

She was in somebody's room.
I don't know what happened.
What happened?"

An old woman is crying. (She always cries.)
She does not live in this lane.
Through her empty mouth she utters gutterals.
"Was ist los?"
"Menschen . . . Haus."
I walk her to her lane. She is crying. She is speaking
in words that sound German.
I knew I studied German for a reason.
She is Dutch, I'm told.
Her memory box full of family smiles.
She is crying when I leave.

Stanzas In Meditation V

I tell Mom I am leaving.
"For good?"

--Wednesday, June 2, 2010

Alzheimer/Albrecht: Losing Is / Is Not / Art

Alzheimer:

alt = old
als = as
al = all
heim = home
er = he

The google book about Alzheimer has random gaps: omission
or forgetting or a sales pitch. I buy the book, *Alzheimer: Life of
a Career and a Disease*, by Konrad & Ulrike Maurer, published
in Germany in 1998 and by Columbia University Press in 2003.
It is worth having, if for Figure 5.6 alone: "Alzheimer jumping
rope." He is seen from the back. His jacket has caught the air like a
petticoat; his arms extend like wings; one leg missing, the one he has
just guided over the rope extended by two women and a girl in long
dresses.

His voice comes to us mostly in questions. He asks them of his
patients. What is your name? *What is your husband's name? What
year is it? 5 x 7 is what? What am I holding in my hand? Where are
you?* Sometimes the answers work, often they do not, like bad
keys. Sometimes the answer is that I was born this year. Some-
times the answer is I don't know. Sometimes the answer is I'm
going to die. *When did you get married?* To which: "indeed, the
woman lives on the same corridor."

Alzheimer's: to discover is to own. The Amerigo Vespucci of
forgetting. His exquisitely drawn maps of neurofibrils and brain
plaque. An exactitude that meets its unraveling in "softness of
the brain."

Auguste D. was his dinghy, his craft, his vessel, the container ship
to his idea. Auguste D. was jealous of her husband, a railroad
clerk, forgot how to cook, screamed constantly, soiled herself, lost
weight. When she died, he received her brain; he drew its tendrils,
its blockages, its shrinkage. On her last day she "was very loud,"
was "very dazed," had ulcerated skin, pneumonia in both lobes.
She died at quarter to 6. She had been ill for four and a half years.

Her husband could not make his payments at the end. Dr. Alois
Alzheimer paid.

With her free hand,
she swats at me, screams,
Stop it. Leave me here to die.

That was the day Malaika King Albrecht's mother forgot how
to get out of the car. Al = all. Brecht = alienation of the audience,
Bertolt. Durer: endure, duration.

Then she cusses, such a string of words.
For a moment I'm almost glad
she remembers them. (17)

There is little art to this losing. Losing objects, losing loved ones,
these are artful. Losing your bedroom, losing the name for puppy,
losing control of the car: these are not. What once was there is
gone. What once was there reappears: "Learn to see dead family
members / in the dark. Over / and over, call to them." (25)
While those of us who cannot see the dead must learn to forget,
too. "Sometimes I / start to dial your number / before I remember."
(35)

The final section of King Albrecht's small book is "Erasure,"
where some of the poems already printed in the text are
re-presented. The words are lighter, they are disappearing, save
for a few bold ones, like "my mother" and *can't get back* and
"Remember?" The poet cannot completely let her language go.
There are still words where erasure is being enacted. Let them
go. Erase them. They are gone. Yet their interference assures us
there is no new poem, no *Rad I Os* to *Paradise Lost*, just occasional
blurts of sense gathered from out the white noise. Forgetting is
not clean, or quiet.

Other absences, elisions: Alzheimer's colleague, Dr. Rudin. First
mention on page 109: "The second scientific assistant, Swiss-born
Ernst Rudin, because full professor of psychiatry in Munich in
1933 and a member of the specialist advisory council for popula-
tion and racial policy in the Third Reich's Interior Ministry; he
can be considered a pioneer of German 'Hereditary and Racial
Care.'" (109)

Second mention: "As a scientist he distinguished himself primar-
ily with works on the genealogy of schizophrenia. However, he
continues to be remembered for writing the medical commentary
on the Nazi law on the prevention of congenitally ill offspring, a
law he also helped to implement."

Pioneer
Remembered

The ethics--the lack thereof--in these terms astonishes.

--Thursday, June 10, 2010

Note: Malaika King Albrecht, *Lessons in Forgetting*, Main Street
Rag, 2010.

Bike Ride: Dementia Meditation (De-meditation)

The problem is not dying; the problem is not dying. The phrase
has run through my head for days now, like a prosody exercise
with bite (over-bite).

Startled four good-sized tan and black piglets along Kamehameha
Highway before He`eia Pier. They turned and ducked into the
brush, wagging their little tails.

One small blue sandal on the shoulder of Kahekili. Left or right?

Google search that lands on this blog: *dementia patient does not
know difference between 2 hours and 2 minutes;* a second wonders
about links between cheese and Alzheimer's.

Birds singing from a monkey pod at the corner of Kahekili and
Hui Iwa as the light waits to change. *Where's the change?* my
Republican interlocutor demanded on the plane. Said environ-
mentalists were to blame for the Gulf disaster; they forced the oil
companies to drill in deep water. Otherwise, they'd drill on land.
Our mothers-with-dementia stories matched.

Katy Butler writes in the *NY Times* that she and her mother
turned off her demented father's pacemaker. It kept him alive,
a perverted fountain of youth. Teresias with a tiny engine in his
chest. Sudden death is out of fashion these days. We insist that
our good-byes go on, and on, and on.

No one has found the line between what we are willing to
concede and what we cannot any longer resist. It's the border
between legal and alien territories, between the place where
they do not ask for ID and the place where they will not accept
it. It's somewhere before or after the keys are taken away or the
3 a.m. wanderings begin or the CIA has implanted a mic in your
forehead. When you reach the border, you are no longer capable
of refusing yourself entry. Fantasies of carbon dioxide forgotten.
You cannot remember to have killed yourself.

Verbs peel away, as if you are slowly forgetting French, volume
by volume of grammar exercises. The past is not simple or

conditional or subjunctive. It cannot be conjugated. There is absence
in the present tense before that, also, ducks away. Scattershot nouns,
processed with unaffiliated verbs, pesto of pine and saw dust.

The cat turns on the phone by lying on it. Sangha called 911
when he was 15 months old. *Someone at your number called. Is
there an emergency?* She found joy in noticing the stones, the
daffodils. She found joy in noticing them again. She found joy.
There was an instant, unremembered. Past that now, she
"dwindles," dies passively.

"Mom," I wanted to say, "I'm ready to give up if you are."
Instead, I asked if I could kiss her cheek. She said yes. Soft.

--Monday, June 21, 2010

Note: Katy Butler, "What Broke My Father's Heart." *New York
Times* (June 18, 2010).

Telephone Call

What are you doing, mom?

Listening to you.

I hear you fell and hurt your elbow.

Oh no, I'm fine.

(She coughs. Coughs again. Again.)

I'm fine. (High-pitched wail this time.)

--Saturday, July 24, 2010

Toward a Documentary Poem about Alzheimer's Care and the Carlyle Group

As part of our ongoing efforts to continuously improve upon our level of service and convenience to you and your loved one, we are making changes to our billing timeline and procedures.

Carlyle was ranked in 2007 as the largest private equity firm in the world . . . however, the firm moved down to second largest as of May 2010.

TOLEDO, Ohio, December 21, 2007—Manor Care, Inc. (NYSE:HCR) today announced that global private equity firm The Carlyle Group has completed its $6.3 billion acquisition of Manor Care . . . "We are pleased with this successful outcome," said Mr. Ormond. "We look forward to working with Carlyle and continuing to provide quality care to our patients and residents."

There are many family members who share our concerns & are eager to work together and do all we can to assure that our family members receive the best care possible. We took the liberty of including your email address in the "Family Council" distribution list. We hope that this hasn't created a problem. Even though you're far away & unable to participate directly, we thought that you would want to be kept abreast of what's going on.

Dunkin Donuts
Baskin-Robbins
Water Pik
Hertz
United Defense Industries (maker of the XM2001 Crusader self-propelled howitzer)
Small Smiles Dental Centers
Synagro Technologies, Inc.
Allison Transmission
Manor Care

On December 18, 2007 David Rubenstein, representing the Carlyle Group, purchased the Magna Carta (one of seventeen copies) at Sotheby's Auction House in New York City. He paid the Perot Foundation $21.3 million.

* (52)"To any man whom we have deprived or dispossessed of
lands, castles, liberties, or rights, without the lawful judgement
of his equals, we will at once restore these. In cases of dispute the
matter shall be resolved by the judgement of the twenty-five bar-
ons referred to below in the clause for securing the peace (§ 61).
In cases, however, where a man was deprived or dispossessed
of something without the lawful judgement of his equals by our
father King Henry or our brother King Richard, and it remains in
our hands or is held by others under our warranty, we shall have
respite for the period commonly allowed to Crusaders, unless a
lawsuit had been begun, or an enquiry had been made at our or-
der, before we took the Cross as a Crusader. On our return from
the Crusade, or if we abandon it, we will at once render justice in
full."

Directors of one of the world's largest armament companies are
planning on meeting in Lisbon in three weeks time. The American
based Carlyle Group is heavily involved in supplying arms to the
Coalition forces fighting in the Iraqi war.

A dementia patient at an Urbana nursing home was raped by
another resident in July but wasn't taken to a hospital for more
than 24 hours, a state investigation found. (10/2007)

Dave Regan, the union's president, said private equity firms that
buy nursing-home chains commonly reduce staffing to increase
profits, causing residents to suffer. *The New York Times* reported
last month that residents of nursing homes bought out by large
Wall Street investment companies wind up with worse care. But
Ullman, of the Carlyle Group, dismissed the union's "smear
and fear campaign" as an attempt to attract employees into the
union. SEIU has 1,100 members among the 60,000 employees
of HCR Manor Care. "This is about gaining more dues-paying
members for the union. It's not about quality of care," he said.

On my last visit, I noticed that the place was under-staffed and
the caregivers were highly stressed. There were a lot of little crises
and not enough caregivers to watch over everyone. One family
member noted that the families are worried that their loved ones
are not being adequately hydrated, as there are not enough staff to
help them eat and drink.

WE, THE EMPLOYEES OF HCR MANORCARE, BELIEVE
THAT OUR RESIDENTS AND PATIENTS AS WELL AS THEIR
FAMILIES

10 are the lifeblood of our business.

C. The rights and responsibilities of residents shall be printed in at least twelve-point type and posted conspicuously in a public place in all assisted living facilities.

"There are the large windows & sunshine."

--Saturday, July 24, 2010

To an Old Philosopher Dying in a Nursing Home

Every 70 seconds, someone in America develops Alzheimer's.
By mid-century, someone will develop the disease every 33 seconds.
You must use the word "develop" in the negative only; do not develop
your thesis or your mind; do not develop your property. To develop
is to clarify. To clarify is to render clear, like a face born out of a chemical

bath. I want to see the hinge between the 70th and 71st, or between
the 33rd and 34th seconds: did Rose (98) pause in mid-sentence, as if
from the coherence of "I'm going to the store" did not follow "to buy milk
and eggs," rather a side-snarl to her sibling dead in 1958? If art's
autonomy cannot be separated from its social effects because the turn

of the sentence has fallen away, comma skittering like a leaf on uncertain
ground, where ground meets ocean or ocean reef, then the clouds that waft
over this nursing home have flown somewhere and someone remembers them
in their vanishing and reconciliation, parallels marked as such only if you
see them in the twin poles of Bill (83)'s walker or in the fork and knife

at Elizabeth (78)'s setting, before she uses one to cut at the other. Just
a warning, Edith (89) is in one of her states today, and we're not taling
geography. The 85-years-and-older population currently includes about
2.4 million people with Alzheimer's disease, or 47 percent of the Azheimer
population aged 65 and over. The threshold, ManorCare, and that more

merciful ManorCare beyond, where buildings are remembered and this
sitting room with its stuffed chairs and large television, its railings
and accessible restrooms, its caregivers (90% of them women), its carpet
comforts, blurs into the place you were where others knew you but
you did not, and Ethel (91) spoke constantly but to no one present and
   Martha (92)

never spoke and to no one present and the present was a board on which
they shuffled, if they walked at all, toward the blurring "distinction between
death *with* dementia and death *from* dementia" that lodges itself in the lungs
while 12.5 billion hours of care were provided in 2009 alone, where even a
small state like Rhode Island held within itself 44.6 million hours of unpaid

care; these hours deepen as the patient's condition worsens, until 24 hour
care must sometimes be mandated by the family with a certificate of guard-
ianship from the state. "I guess no one will fight over this estate," the
  judge said,
on seeing that the plaintiff was an only child. To fight one needs to have one's
wits about, which doesn't say much for wits. I write in memory of hers,

though my memory creases over time, de-creases, which is not to say I fear
losing it but that your face cannot coexist with the name I once uttered for it,
nor can the name answer to the idea I gave to it, grace note to the 454,000
new cases this year and to the relatives for whom this means being known
less as themselves than as a falling away, a loan held against death,

monthly check (to the tune of $6,000) for room and board and hair styling
and medical care. It is a kind of total disruptiveness at the end, with every
visible thing diminished and yet there is still a bed, a chair, a common room
for conversation, a nursing station, and a nook with benches for sitting on:
The moving walkway is now ending. Watch your step.

  --debts to Wallace Stevens and Alzheimer's Association Report 2010

When Does Life End? A Multiple Choice Test

Politics and dysfunction are not the sole province of English departments, soccer clubs, or the U.S. Senate. Her Alzheimer's home, too, is going through a period of turmoil. So "Corporate" (as everyone calls it, which means ManorCare, which means Carlyle) has stepped in, replaced the Director of her home, and we hope for the best.

We hope for the best. In my mother's case, I no longer know what best is. As my conversation with her current social worker ended this morning, she told me, almost as afterthought, that an orthopedic surgeon reported that she has several breaks in her elbow, but that she's not a candidate for surgery. That they should watch for symptoms of pain. That she is not exhibiting them now. (Not in pain from a severely and multiply fractured elbow?)

So I told the social worker about the problems I'd noticed--too few staff to cover dinnertime and sundowning chaos at the same time; overheard complaints about management, and so on. But I added that, while my mother had had a couple of years in which a flower could bring her joy ten times in five minutes, she does not seem to feel that now. That I hope for release. It felt odd, even dangerous, to say that.

Later in the day I found Atul Gawande's essay in The New Yorker via Daily Kos. It's titled, "Letting Go: What should medicine do when it can't save your life?" He writes about how hard it is for him--a surgeon--to know what the term "dying" means, since medical interventions keep people alive so long past the point they would have died a century ago. Some quotations from the piece resonate:

For all but our most recent history, dying was typically a brief process. Whether the cause was childhood infection, difficult childbirth, heart attack, or pneumonia, the interval between recognizing that you had a life-threatening ailment and death was often just a matter of days or weeks.

Later:

*Dying used to be accompanied by a prescribed set of customs. . .
Reaffirming one's faith, repenting one's sins, and letting go of one's
worldly possessions and desires were crucial, and the guides provided
families with prayers and questions for the dying in order to put them
in the right frame of mind during their final hours. Last words came to
hold a particular place of reverence.*

As a formalist measure of dying, last words put an end to a story
that can then be told from beginning, middle, end, or some usual
crazy patchwork of all three. Hence:

*"Is she dying?" one of the sisters [of a terminally ill woman] asked me.
I didn't know how to answer the question. I wasn't even sure what the
word "dying" meant anymore. In the past few decades, medical science
has rendered obsolete centuries of experience, tradition, and language
about our mortality, and created a new difficulty for mankind: how to
die.*

Gawanda writes about a woman, a specialist in end of life issues,
who went back to her father's sickbed to ask him questions that
she herself wanted to avoid. When asked what quality of life
meant to him, he responded that he wanted to be able to eat
chocolate and watch a football game. When called upon to de-
cide if the next treatment was worth the risk or not (in their case,
it was, and it worked), that was all she needed to know. Many
cases do not have that ending, or any ending.

In 1991, according to the article, medical leaders came up with
questions for the very ill. They were:

1. Do you want to be resuscitated if your heart stops?
2. Do you want aggressive treatments such as intubation and
mechanical ventilation?
3. Do you want antibiotics?
4. Do you want tube or intravenous feeding if you can't eat on
your own?

But even these simple questions elicit complicated answers. My
mother gets antibiotics for her occasional pneumonias. She is not
dying, she has dementia. While she has often failed to feed

Mother News

Chapter One

Susan:

I was surprised not to find Martha sitting in her chair in the TV
room. I was told she's been going to Activities so I went there
to check on her. She looked tired. Her hair needed to be done.
She was not in a congenial mood. Perhaps I had woken her. We
talked for a little while and then I went to speak with Emma the
nurse. Emma said that Martha has been eating better and gained
a couple of pounds. She was stable and aging in place. She was
due to get her hair done soon.
Hope this helps.

--September 4, 2010

Chapter Two

Dear Susan:

Martha was in the living room sitting next to 2 people. I gave her
a hearty hello and when I said "hello girlfriend" she laughed.
One of the people sitting next to her was Janice, the same name
as me. Kidding around, I said "her name is Janice, my name is
Janice what is your name?" Martha answered, Janice. A couple of
minutes later I asked her her name and she said she didn't know.
(She was serious). I think Martha when called by that name will
answer, but she can't identify herself as Martha.

I then touched her nails and said how beautiful they looked. She
snapped them away. I forgot that she does not like to be touched
in any way. I apologized and repeated how beautiful her nails
looked. The aide said that everything is status quo. Martha
occasionally goes to an activity but its less than more. Before I
left, Martha said everythings fine.

--Saturday, September 4, 2010

Are you my mother?

Martha (92) was once a jay, the kind that chases cats, children, eats your eggs; in old age, she is finch, sparrow, slender bird who misplaced her song on a bank of reeds, for whom the Second War was an oboe played unto forgetting.

Martha lost her mother, her nest, her song, set out to find her Henrietta in the common room, the dining room, the corridor, in every cranny of her home. But all she found was an Edna (90) and a Mildred (89) and an Edith (95) and a Rose (90); none of them resembled her, as they were old. "Are you my mother?" Martha asked them each, and they said no, they were not hers but someone else's mother, sister, aunt, niece. "I took care of you," one said, "but I am not your mother; look at me, I am tall and you are short; my hair is gray and yours is white; my eyes are brown and yours so blue."

Martha wondered if the bulldozer was her mother, or the ambulance, or the collie. She wondered if the air-conditioner was her mother, or the heater in winter, if the clothes on the line were left by mother, if the woman who did her hair was her mother, if Betty or Christine or Amber were her mother. Someone fed her still. Someone laid out her clothes on the narrow bed. Someone took her to the bathroom after lunch. Someone turned on the television in the morning, and turned it off at night. Someone kept trying to hug her, though she refused.

The story ends when the little bird finds her mother is a bear. The bear takes her home, where she finds siblings in the pig, the hippo, the alligator, and they all eat apple pie. But Martha can't find herself in that story. She is bird and she is bear, but she is also orphan. The end is not the beginning, is not an end, is an ongoing whose plot cannot find the door, the bed, the chair. Happily ever.

--After Are You My Mother and A Mother for Choco

Mother news: "She had a dog in her past."

Dear Susan:

Martha was sitting in the living room not doing anything. I came today with a stuffed dog which was quite cuddly. When I offered it to Martha she immediately took it out of my hand s and wrapped her arms around it. When I asked her if she had a name she said she did but unfortunately said it so low I couldn't hear it. I stayed for awhile and pet the dog with her. She told me that she had a dog in the past. I hope this gives her some joy.

Martha's weight is stable and she continues to carry on the same.

————————

Yes, she had a dog to whom she gave many names. I wish I could remember them all, recite them with the same delight she took in chanting them to me. The sequence included a creek in western Pennsylvania and ended with "O'Mallory O'Keefe." The portrait of two dogs above is signed with her maiden name, M. Keefe, '38, which would have been the year before she graduated from college. In the dogs' eyes you can see something of her wit.

My mother's mother had her dog put to sleep while my mother
was away. The deed was unforgivable. I do not know that it was
the same dog, a collie.

———————————

I found the creek by googling "creeks near Meadville." It's the
Cussewego.

So it was, perhaps, Cussewego O'Mallory O'Keefe, except there
was yet another name, a first name. Neither I nor my computer
remember that.

--Monday, November 22, 2010

Telephone Conversations with my Mother

--Hello. The weather's fine. I'm eating. Good to hear from you and to know that you're ok.

The breathing, sensing body draws its sustenance and its very substance from the soils, plants, and elements that surround it . . . it is very difficult to discern, at any moment, precisely where this living body begins and where it ends. (46)

--Hello. Good to hear from you and to know that you're ok.

We can experience things--can touch, hear, and taste things--only because, as bodies, we are ourselves included in the sensible field, and have our own textures, sounds, and tastes. (68)

--Hello. Good to hear from you and know that everything's ok.

[I]t is primarily through my engagement with what is not me that I effect the integration of my senses, and thereby experience my own unity and coherence. (125)

--Hello, hello, I can't hear you.

Prior to the spread of writing, ethical qualities like "virtue," "justice," and "temperance" were thoroughly entwined with the specific situations in which those qualities were exhibited. . . Arising in specific situations, they were inseparable from the particular persons or actions that momentarily embodied them. (110)

--H e l l o?

In the waters that surge in waves against the distant edge of the land, still stranger powers, multihued and silent, move in crowds among alien forests of coral and stone . . . (49)

--Monday, December 27, 2010

Note: Italicized language from David Abram's *The Spell of the Sensuous: Perception and Language in a More-Than-Human World.* NY: Vintage, 1996.

Lovebirds

[Alzheimer's home, midday.]

Gloria (a new woman) and Ed (a familiar man) sit on the couch together.

--I miss my family. Do you miss yours? Do you miss your son? Do you have a good relationship?

--I don't know.

--You haven't seen him in a long time. But you love him and he you. Men don't always express affection; that's how it is.

--He's 30 or 40. Married? I don't believe so.

--Who does he look like? Does he look like you?

--He's somewhat balding.

--Were you happily married?

--Of course.

--Yes or no? Were you? Quite?

--Yes.

____

--The day is a little bit dark.
--No it isn't. (So says a woman in gray and black sweater who keeps gesturing at her own breasts.)

____

--They locked the door to my room. I want to go lie down in my room. I can go lie in my room and you can go lie in yours. They don't want us to touch each other. Don't make them separate us!

--Frankly, I don't give a shit.

--They don't want us to touch, but I like it. You love me, don't you?

--You bet I do. My sweetheart. I'll kick their teeth in.

A man in space talks of the harm we do with irresponsible words. His sister-in-law was shot in Arizona.

--I've never been intimate with anyone except the one I was married to. He died. Would you like to live with me?

--Very much so.

[Joe says "36."]

--I want to lie down. I have no secrets. My room is locked. Southern girls need their rest. I'd like to hold you, scratch your hair a little bit.

--Would you like to marry me?

--Yes, I like your touch.

--But you don't want to marry me?

--Yes, I want you very badly.

--Only if you love me.

--I love you, you know that.

--It's a deal!!!!

--I feel very lucky knowing you. I feel God brought us together, don't you? I want to get in my room!!

Joe notices me in a chair: "cetta persona!!!" Turns out he delivered the *New York Post* in Brooklyn. Speaks Italian, as much as he speaks.

Caretakers L & Betty laugh about the love birds. L says she's going to find love here too, one day. She has a bad toothache, wants soup so she can take Tylenol. Her ex wanted her back, but she said no. She's going to find love. Won't have to do the cooking. She says this as she sorts through a library of pill sheets, takes notes on them. Betty prays everyday she doesn't end up like them. She does not want to lose her mind.

Love happens all the time here. Sometimes the men's wives get very upset. *I never want to see him with that woman ever again,* they'll say. They don't understand the disease, L says.

Bonanza is on TV. A woman falls for a man and they decide to marry. His name is Frank, but he is not. He lies to her. She is stricken by grief. Another man died on the eve of her wedding to him, and now this. Before she is betrayed she tells him: *But when you love someone, what they've been or done in the past doesn't matter.* But then it does.

Ed approaches his love, who is now lying on the couch, her bad leg out on a chair. She is calm. When she beckons him, he leans to hug her, his face bright. He has a fresh stain on the front of his gray running pants. *You dropped some water on your pants, she tells him, you should go change them.*

There are crutches for all of us, the star tells Emily, who lies stricken on her bed. You had the crutch of grief for all those years, and he had the crutch of lying. He has had humiliation and courage both. And you will not marry him now?

They meet in the dusty town square. She tells him she still loves
him, wants to marry him. He is surprised, but he does not leave.
They get into the carriage and ride off, as the credits begin to
scroll. They are happy again. They are getting married. *You were
always a man of action, Frank,* the star says to the man.

My mother sits through these scenes, quiet, face tilted toward
the television. She is the still point in the room. She is wearing a
San Miguel de Allende teeshirt and needs new slacks; her brown
ones are coming apart at what seams are left. She smiles and says
thank you. Sylvia's son says that means she understands things.
Do I agree? he asks. No, I say, I think it's just that she likes you.

--Tuesday, January 11, 2011

Soap Opera Generator

*11/13/2007, WASHINGTON—Retired Justice Sandra Day
O'Connor's husband, who suffers from Alzheimer's, has found a new
romance, and his happiness is a relief to his wife, an Arizona TV report
reveals.*

Rose (98) stalks the paranoid man, of indeterminate age,
while Mildred (89) bids a tearful farewell to Bob (95)
in the middle of a citywide blackout. Emma (89)
decides to go after Tom (85) but as she turns to leave
she finds the door locked, the keypad a mystery,
so Agnes (90) shoots Betty the caregiver, before
the plot can be foiled by Anne, the administrator,
and Edith (98) fools Martha (92), demanding the dollar
it takes to ride a bus from this city to Paris, where
she lives; nearby, on Bliss Lane in the county of
Fairfax, beside the Confederates' highway, Bill (76)
obsesses over the surry with the fringe on top as
Xander, the moderator, shifts to the current events
of 1985, when President Reagan still remembered
his own name and Min (79) gets drunk, wakes up with
Bill (67) who still gets it up, and the con men descend
on the care home to steal the paintings and raid the safe,
while delivery men drop off Depends and Ensure,
until Rose (98) stops stalking the paranoid man, who was
worried about it, and Anne (80) who was a professional
pianist, tries to remember the lyrics to Frank Sinatra
songs while the truth will out about Martha (92) who stuck
her family photos in the drawer, and Bill (67 & 76) who would
give her flowers if he could get through the padlocks,
and Agnes (90) who suffers a fit of remorse for her actions
as the romantic picnic in the lunch room begins,
with the cloth napkins and real glasses, the chairs
scraping linoleum as in a love story to which we will
later affix a soundtrack, more strings than horns, more
horns than drums, and Ethel (87) discovers who was the
real grandfather of her grandchild and endures a shotgun
wedding with Bill (76) and they live happily ever after
in legal wedded bliss. The End.

Going Home

Fred Wah:

*This notion that home can operate as a foundation of identity allows
that identity (since we seem to need it) might function as some kind of
"soul," part of the baggage we can't leave (behind, or somewhere else)
and that it (identity) therefore needs the constructs of home (place,
workplace, school, kitchen, neighborhood, and so forth) eventually, in
dementia, as a presence that is absent.*

One of my mother's caregivers says there are two things the
residents never forget, sexual desire and home. They all remember
where they come from, she says. And my mother? I ask. If she
were more expressive, yes.

Ed kisses Sylvia's fingers at lunch, thanks her. Her breath is a
dusk engine, its gears too audible for comfort. She is loud: she
belches, she yells out what she does not want. Luckily, Gloria
who keeps asking Ed if he has a line of girls waiting for him to
get out, fails to notice; she is too busy eating. Her long hair is
white underneath a mottled orange.

Gloria wants to help clean up after lunch, but drops the first
thing she picks up.

Janice shows up to check on my mother. We talk about how little
response we get from her, how oddly stable she has been over
the last couple of years, how she does not know us, how she will
not get out of her chair. When Janice kneels next to mom's chair,
mom's face lights up. Yes, she will take a walk. We flank her, take
her elbows and walk her to her room. From outside, I gesture
in and say, there's a picture of Fred in there. Do you remember
Fred? Oh yes, I remember Fred, she says, and smiles. Then the
long trek back to the common area. Bonanza is on. Another scene
of justice or betrayal.

Do you have more kleenexes? I need more kleenexes, says Gloria.
I keep losing my urine.

Those who remember their children's names will tell you. He's
a good kid. Sometimes I wanna wring his neck, but he's a good
kid. I never done it yet. Her mind isn't right, she says. She makes
circles next to her head. *Meshugah.*

We lose our fluids. We lose our thoughts. We lose our minds. But
we do not, it seems, lose that sense of home, even when we cannot
express it. *Are you going to take me home?* is one of the most fre-
quent questions overheard here. *I want to go home now. I miss home.*

--Friday, January 14, 2011

Note: Fred Wah's words are from his blog on dementia at
http://fjwah.wordpress.com/

1/14/11: Headlines

96 year old woman calls in death threat to federal judge from
her nursing home bed; he leaves work early, deputy by his side

Man has violent argument with self in a mirror; tries to strangle
caretaker

Sylvia says she has a home but does not know where it is; "can
you tell me what I'm doing here?" she asks

96 year old woman calls her guardian to wish him a Merry
Christmas, then adds, "but YOU people don't celebrate the
birth of our Lord, do you?"

According to Gloria, her sore knee is a mystery, because she
has not been playing football lately

Get the retirement you deserve (the happiest times of our lives
are with family and friends) by taking out a reverse mortgage

When the police ask her about her threat against the judge, the
96 year old woman says, "you bet I'll kill that son of a bitch!"

Love in the Time of Alzheimer's

[Ed & Gloria snuggle on the couch:]

Ed: Arm in arm & hand in hand!
I must stay with you.

Gloria: If you get too affectionate, they'll speak to me. They did
before. Maybe I should take you to your room.

[Ed murmurs in Gloria's ear, fondles her]

Gloria: We're in a public place. You're very special to me. Can I
take you to your room so you can lie down? That might help.

Ed: [holds her hand and arm] It's you. You're my babe. You're
the one. No one can take you.

Gloria: No one's going to take you away from me.

Ed: I have the right to love you.

————————————————

Sylvia: [again, again] What am I doing here? Why Virginia? I live
in New York. The Bronx.

When asked to sit to watch a movie, Sylvia replies that she's not
interested.

When I say to Sylvia, we keep seeing each other, she says: *I'm not
tired of YOUR face.*

————————————————

Gloria: What do you want to do this year?

Ed: Explore each other.

Gloria: And then what?

Ed: Explore each other for a year and then work on love. Love making.

Gloria: I haven't made love in many years. I was a good Southern girl, didn't fool around. Why don't you talk to me?

Ed: I have not found many girls who want to experiment. They have been trained to expect that. They have been the aggressors.

Gloria: You fooled around a lot?

Ed: I played the games they wanted me to play.

Gloria: But you could've gotten AIDS!! You let girls take advantage of you? How long ago?

Ed: Years & years & years ago. I put it completely out of my mind.

Gloria: I didn't fool around. Oh, it's hot. I had a very happy social life. In the South, it's very different from up here. I was a good girl. You dress too warmly for a Yankee. I'm a southern shit. Not toots, chick.

Ed: Chickenshit.

Gloria: At A___ there were six or seven men to every girl. There were big bands. I love to dance! I taught dance down South, then came to DC. Taught elementary school. Never fooled around.

But I bet you had a happy life & the girls took advantage of you.

Ed: I don't know.

Gloria: I don't share my goodies with anyone unless they're special. You're my buddy.

Gloria Are you a happy man?

Ed: Sure.

Gloria: All the time, or now & then?

Ed: Now and then.

Gloria: Better to be silly than sad.

Ed: I agree.

———————————————

Gloria: I should go lie down again. [They kiss.]

Will you come see me when I go home?
You could sleep on the couch in the living room.
Would you like your own bedroom?
Would you like to sleep with me?

Ed: I'd rather sleep with you.

Gloria: We'd have to be married first!
You need a shampoo. Your head is oily.

I have a waiting list.
I'm teasing you, I hope you know.

———————————————

Gloria: Are you married? Are you sure you're not married?

Ed: I would know.

Gloria: One of the ladies said you were married.

Ed: Then ask HER.

———————————————

Gloria: You don't want to live here the rest of your life?

Ed: What brought that on?
Look out the window. There are trees. I suppose not.

Gloria: Not in a facility. You should live the life you want. God made you perfect, in his likeness. There is nothing wrong with you. You ought to be living the life you're meant to live.

Are you happy?

Ed: I suppose so. I don't know what you want to hear.

Gloria: I was raised in a talking family.

When you come to my house, I'd like to shampoo & cut your hair. I'll be going home soon, & I'll miss you.

Ed: I don't know what you're getting at!!

Gloria: Say something nice to me before I leave.

Ed: I LOVE YOU.

My mother's old neighbors come to visit. He says he's had two episodes of global transient amnesia; says it's something for the blog. They tell mom she looks good, her hair looks good, note that she has a dog, the stuffed one I put on her lap each day; the outside social worker brought it to her. It has big, alien-like eyes. I tell her the dog is Irish, McGuillicutty O'Mallory O'Keefe. They said they came once and took mom's picture. Some neighbors refused even to look at the photograph. They show mom pictures of their kids, their grandkids. The pictures are old, but who's to know? Mom smiles at each image on the back of the neighbor's digital camera. When we leave, the neighbor asks her to wave. He waves good-bye to her, and she waves back. I could do that all day with her, he says.

You should have been more quiet, someone said to her husband
in the parking lot, because the woman on the couch was saying
that her mother committed suicide and her sister, too, so she tries
to keep in good spirits. Who knows if it was true.

All of it is. It's the place where stories start, where they fail to
reach climax or conclusion or denouement or even the end of a
well formed phrase. It's a return to innocence when innocence
is no longer possible. Why stop them? Why keep order in the
house? Why not let the story end with sex, or what they might
remember of it, arms and mouths, legs, the place where she has
lost her urine and his comes out sometimes unawares?

We wouldn't want to tell their children what had happened, one
caregiver explains.

--Saturday, January 15, 2011

Separation Anxieties

Dinner. Sylvia's son and daughter-in-law were leaving; they'd
been putting puzzles together with her while we talked politics.
We walked to the dining room, where the dance begins.

--Where are you going? What am I doing here? I want to go with
you!

Daughter-in-law leaves (as cover). Son starts to leave. Sylvia
gets up and follows. Ma, I gotta leave now, he says, or you won't
believe what trouble I'll be in.

--I don't care! she says.

--I'm going to get a parking ticket, a big one.

--How much is the ticket? I'll pay it.

--$100 dollahs.

--I'll pay the $100 dollahs, she says.

--But really, ma, I gotta go. We'll be back tomorrow.

--What time?

--Afternoon.

A caregiver walks over to talk to Sylvia, who is seated again. Her
son hurries off, though he can't resist greeting each resident by
name as he leaves through the kitchen.

This evening I said good-bye to my mother for now. For now.
The woman down the hall was "agitated." Her daughter said
it was her time; I heard the word "hospice" as I walked past.
Passed by. There's a line in Elizabeth Bishop about past and
passing, as if they were conjugations of the same verb. Past and
passing and to come--perhaps.

Her neighbor at dinner never speaks, was a translator from
Chinese. When she saw my mother's stuffed dog, she laughed
out loud. When Sylvia saw the stuffed bear later, she said, I'm
not scayed of dat! I sold those in my stoah. She poked its nose.
She swatted her son with her napkin.

Mom has been more lucid on this visit than on the last, in May.
She smiles, she nods, she says yes when yes is called for, no
when no is appropriate. Before I leave she says she does not
want the bear. No bear.

I say good-bye to the others. I say farewell to Janice, who pets
the dog's tail, good-bye to the lovebirds on the couch, good-bye
to Estella, who rumbles behind her walker, good-bye to Florence,
to Tia, to Sylvia. They cluster around me, touch my clothes, the
ones who are up. They talk to me in bursts. *You fixed it,* says
Florence, when I get the snaps right on my jacket. I'm tired. I
want to go home to Hawai'i, which is so far away and where the
weather is always so good. I do not want to leave them behind.
Let behind be now, and again now, and again.

I'll be back in a few months, I say to mom.

--Saturday, January 15, 2011

80

Misreading Oren Izenberg

While in Washington D.C. a few days ago, I picked up Oren
Izenberg's *Being Numerous: Poetry and the Ground of Social Life*. I'm
reading the book unfaithfully, not following Izenberg's argument
so much as translating it into my own thoughts on writing about
dementia. Pardon my misprisions; they're all I've got.

Izenberg is interested in history, but not historicism, poetry but
not craft or form. Although his canon is, shall we say, canonical
(Yeats, Oppen, O'Hara, the Language writers), he's more inter-
ested in noems, or non-poems, than in poetry as poetry. "The
persistent production of non-poems asks that we entertain the
notion that what the poet intends by means of poetry is not the
poem," he argues early on (12). The ground on which Izenberg
bases his reading of these non-poems is personhood. Everything
we usually consider about poems in the classroom passes away
in Izenberg's writing about poetry not as an art but as an
investigation of personhood.

My first desire was to identify with his argument; here at last, I
surmised, was a writer less interested in form than in meaning,
less interested in the structure of poems than in their confronta-
tions with existence. In his own terms, Izenberg is less interested
in the conversations people have about poems (as he illustrates
in the last chapter) than in the ways in which poems create rela-
tionship within the reader, "reorient the person toward a shared
world." People are not persons, but persons matter desperately
to him.

This desire for identification is not met by Izenberg's thesis. But I
found a relationship of fruitful misreading in the last paragraph
of his introduction. Writing about Alzheimer's, as I do, is nothing
if not writing about personhood, what it is, how it alters, remains,
how much it depends--or does not depend --on reciprocity and
"reading." It's writing about existence at the point at which
existence is called into question. So I'd like to quote extensively
from Izenberg's last paragraph, and then talk to it, person to
person-like:

OI: "Poems, like persons, are always going about some business of their own, which in the moment seems much more urgent-- and certainly more specifiable than the business of being instances of what they generally, abstractly, essentially are. If the particular business of individual persons is what we mean by living, then the specification of the business of poems is what we generally mean by reading" (38).

SMS: But you assume, Oren, that persons are those who have "particular business," which suggests means and ends. By putting persons in parallel with poems, you are further suggesting that any two people conducting their business can read poems (together, apart, or even asymmetrically). What of persons who do not have "business," who do not "read" poems, or anything else? What of the woman who sat "reading" the newspaper the other day in my mother's Alzheimer's home, looked at a benign headline in the sports section, and uttered a horrified "oh no!"? I can read her "reading" as the correct response to the wrong communication, perhaps, but she is not reading in the way you or I are reading. My response to her is quite complicated; first I want to know what she is responding to, and then parse out the ways in which she is responding appropriately to a headline that is not in front of her (the murders in Tucson, for example, whether or not she knows about them). At this point it matters more that I know about them, so that her response to the sports headline echoes mine to a different headline. We are in concert, but not concord.

OI: "Taking up debates about collective intentionality within contemporary social philosophy, I propose an alternative to models of poetic community built around conversation, interpretation, or translation. Writing myself into the history of poetic intentions I describe, I also argue for the interest and value (if not necessarily the truth) of a theory of collective intentions that is crucially internalist; it conceives of the ability of forming intentions for partnership-in-action whether or not one has a partner--indeed, whether or not anyone else in the world exists" (38-39).

SMS: I would take that further, because the community I just spent a week living in, or among, or with--the community that comes and goes from the common area in my mother's

Alzheimer's home--is not built around any of these things. Talk is most often solitary (with the current exception of the lovebirds), reasonable interpretation belongs to me but not to them, and translation is often impossible. Lacking language, people fall into mystery, a rather different mystery from the kind that usually cloaks them. So yes, the result is "internalist." The partnership I form in the common room is less common in the larger sense than in the private one. I am partnered with myself. The days are spent in conversation: what happened? what might it have meant? in what ways did it fit with other events of the day, or the background sounds of the television? And yet, I would argue that "anyone else in the world exists."

OI: "The ability to recover--by reading poems--a conviction in even the solitary person's innate and 'primitive' capacity to formulate 'we-intentions' may, I suggest, have a transformative effect on one's felt capacities for relationship, and reorient the person toward a shared world" (39).

SMS: This is true for me when I visit my mother. It is not true for her. I try to read her a poem of Keats that she once loved and she looks away. When I hand her a stuffed dog, however, she lights up. Not a reading of poems, but a reading of relationship with something soft, something with big eyes. That's what matters because something is exchanged between her and--if not quite a being--the material imitation of one.

OI: "The question that the poets in this tradition pose to social thought is of the most fundamental kind: not how to distribute fairly the privileges of identity, but how to secure the ground of identity; not just of how to do things with persons, but how to know that a person is there at all" (39).

SMS: It's not just that I am a postmodernist, perhaps, that I cannot hold to the "ground of identity" in this context. After all, I also live in Hawai`i, where identities are constructed on the `aina. To know Alzheimer's is to know the lack of ground and yet to recognize that there is humanity in its lack, to know that a person is there, if not a personhood. There is no fair distribution of privilege in the Alzheimer's home; there are only shades of self-loss.

Izenberg's last sentence: "how to know that a person is there at all," takes on a new urgency in this context. To write Alzheimer's is to acknowledge that a person is there, even if she cannot read you or your words, even if she cannot know what is said about her (is not writer or audience, in other words). To write Alzheimer's is to acknowledge that the "common room" is, indeed, held in common, even if very few conversations occur there. That the common room is a very social space, even for those who have become internalized by their illness. That poetry, or non-poetry, is the fund of memory that sits alongside the vast swatches of forgetting that inhabit the Alzheimer's home. The subject is forgetting, but the writing is all memory. It's as tangled a tale as Shelley's assertion that art and politics rather miraculously align, an assertion about which Izenberg has much that is valuable to say.

The conclusion to the book is as beautiful as it is sad. Sadder yet when the story of his failed relationship, his failed idea of reading together as relationship, gets translated into the failures of Alzheimer's. One may involve psychology, the other biology, but they are analogous. The book's ending (are there spoiler alerts in literary criticism?), when the devoted reader discovers that his partner in reading had stopped some time back, oddly mirrors the feeling I have in dealing with the Alzheimer's residents. Yes, "Life got in the way." We'll all finish another time.

———————————————

The hospital room, the Alzheimer's home, these are theaters. They are theaters in which the subject is existence itself. What is existence, and is it coming to an end? At what point is existence full and at what point empty? What do all the intermediate states tell us about either end of this frail line?

It was in the theater of my father's last hospital room that I discovered that life at its most extreme (at its end) structures itself like a poem. This may be because I am taught to read by way of poems; perhaps it also resembles engineering, musical composition, landscape design. But my father was speaking poetry. He was speaking the poem in the sense Izenberg means it--it was all about personhood--and in the sense that a poet means it, too--his metaphors had all become true.

In my mother's common room there are scenes upon scenes.
They are not simple scenes, but layered, synchronous. So when
the lovebirds coo to each other on the couch, they echo Bonanza
on the television; when *Animal Planet* runs, my mother pets her
"dog." This is not cause and effect, but synchronicity. The television,
like the residents, relies on clichés for its power; the shows rely on
scenic structures that are none too complicated by themselves (until
they are brought into the same space as common room interactions).
Enclosure, repetition, cliché. And an uncommon honesty, too. This is
not a paradox.

Izenberg's book is not about my mother, but I choose to read it
with and against her existence. I'm glad he writes about persons,
and that I can read what he says about them. I'm also glad that
there are persons outside of poetry, even outside of non-poetry.
To "reorient the person toward a shared world" means that what
we share may be a world of poetry, but that it sometimes exists
far outside our reading of poems.

--Tuesday, January 18, 2011

Note: Oren Izenberg, *Being Numerous: Poetry and the Ground of
Social Life*, Princeton: Princeton University Press, 2011.

Stanzas in Medication

Namenda, 5 Mg tablet: Memantine [Namenda] is used to treat
the symptoms of Alzheimer's disease. Memantine is in a class
of medications called NMDA receptor antagonists. It works by
decreasing abnormal activity in the brain. Memantine can help
people with Alzheimer's disease to think more clearly and
perform daily activities more easily, but it is not a cure and does
not stop the progression of the disease. 60 each. 9.00

Spiriva, Cp-Handihaler: SPIRIVA is a once-daily inhaled mainte-
nance prescription treatment for chronic obstructive pulmonary
disease (COPD). COPD is a serious lung disease that includes
chronic bronchitis, emphysema, or both. SPIRIVA treats both
conditions by opening narrowed airways. 30 each. 9.00

Alendronate Sodium, 70 Mg Tab: Prophylaxis and treatment of
female osteoperosis. 4 each. 3.00

Donepezil, Hcl 10 Mg Tab: Donepezil may improve the ability to
think and remember or slow the loss of these abilities in people
who have AD. However, donepezil will not cure AD or prevent
the loss of mental abilities at some time in the future. 30 each.
3.00

Calcium 600 w/Vit D tab: Before you take calcium and vitamin
D combination, tell your doctor if you have kidney disease, past
or present kidney stones, heart disease, circulation problems, a
parathyroid disorder, or if you are pregnant or breast-feeding. 60
each. 7.10

Micardis, Hct 80-12.5 Mg Tab: FDA has not concluded that ARBs
increase the risk of cancer. The Agency is reviewing information
related to this safety concern and will update the public when
additional information is available. 30 each. 9.00

Losartan-Hetz 100-12.5 Mg Tab: Hypovolemia. Hepatic impair-
ment. Severe CHF (with hypotension or excess volume depletion
by overdiuresis). Diabetes. Renal artery stenosis. Asthma. Post-
sympathectomy. SLE. Gout. Monitor electrolytes. May interfere

with parathyroid tests. Elderly. Pregnancy (Cat.C in 1st trimester). Nursing mothers: not recommended. 30 each. 3.00

Total due: 43.10

--Friday, January 28, 2011

never the chess game the checker game
The words are under control but letters squirm.
Juggler, why need I invent so much
I have searched for potent words

in the back yard tongueless
Words dance away seductively
on the beach in the hissing surf
I don't know don't know I have to be careful

Tyger still burning in me burning
I can spell the word "dying" but I do not know what it means
to become old the innocence I am someone else looking
at me The old man In the mirror Startles Me

But the young man In the photograph
Is stranger Still.
I struggle to spell the word "hour."
And cannot bear to speak Cut my legs off but don't

take away my ability to write. --'You cannot Imagine',
he said, 'What has Been happening To me--'
I am unconsciously mixing words: our and out,
would and wood, me and be.

the saving ray of strangeness
saving ray of exile
ray of darkeness
I will sing until no word is left.

Lost and fearful. I wake up hiccupping with fear.
I dreamed one night *I was in a house near here*
tho I cannot find it. I was lost
and they could not guide me **wandering foreigner**

Alzheimer's is like trying to describe air. the finches
yell us us us us does their language contain them
I must now be done with writing and lick words instead.
whereupon curious archangels begin to watch

--Saturday, January 29, 2011

Note: Arial text comes from Thomas DeBaggio's *Losing My
Mind: An Intimate Look at Life With Alzheimer's* (NY: The Free
Press, 2002). Oppen's Courier words come from *New Collected
Poems* (NY: New Directions, edited by Michael Davidson).

Mother News

Hi:

Martha was in her usual chair slouched to the side. She acknowl-
edged that she knew me and said hello.

Today I read from The Little Prince which had pop ups. She read
back the title to me but when I asked her if she would like to
read some of it she refused. She didn't appear to be interested
too much with the text but did show some interest with the
pop ups so I worked with them. We looked at each pop up and
some of them she smiled. After awhile she appeared restless so
I stopped. I held her hand for a short bit but then she started to
move away.

According to the nurse she has been stable. Occasionally, she
goes to Activities but on a very selected basis.

[J.]

--Thursday, February 24, 2011

Odd Doc Day: The ROE Form for the DOD

For years, I got frequent correspondence from the Department of Defense regarding my mother's marital status. Over and over, I was asked if my mother had remarried. I had to check in a box to say she had not. I added a scrawled note, "my mother has Alzheimer's and is not fit to marry." And then the next month, another one came. And another. Finally, I sent in a copy of my certificate of guardianship, adding that my mother was not capable of remarrying, to please stop sending the request. As of today (not because this arrived today, but because I am cleaning house, so that I know now that I'm late in responding to the request), I received this note. My mother has graduated from someone who might defraud the DOD by remarrying to someone who might assist me in defrauding the DOD by ceasing to exist. I've taken off the header, which includes her social security number.

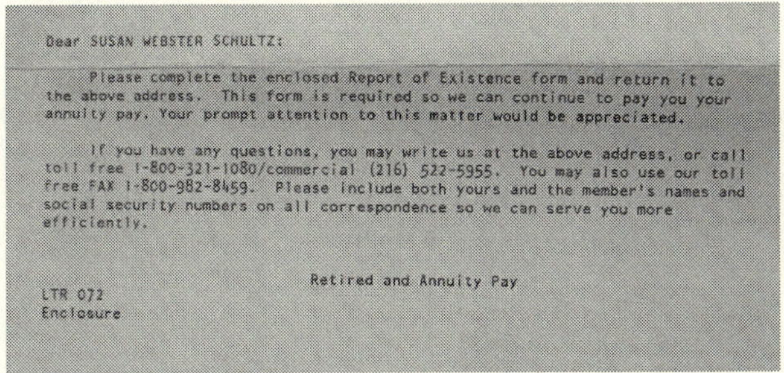

Dear SUSAN WEBSTER SCHULTZ:

Please complete the enclosed Report of Existence form and return it to the above address. This form is required so we can continue to pay you your annuity pay. Your prompt attention to this matter would be appreciated.

If you have any questions, you may write us at the above address, or call toll free 1-800-321-1080/commercial (216) 522-5955. You may also use our toll free FAX 1-800-982-8459. Please include both yours and the member's names and social security numbers on all correspondence so we can serve you more efficiently.

Retired and Annuity Pay

LTR 072
Enclosure

This is called the "Report of Existence Form," one that assures them, not that she is alive, but that she exists. Her "life" (is there a "Report of Life" form?) has been edited down to the size of a form. She is not living what we refer to as a "full life" (ah, Lakoff & Johnson, your containers are showing). No, this is about money, after all. If you exist, you get your late husband's pension. If you no longer exist, the money runs dry.

I will write a note to say that yes, my mother is still alive, thank you. I will put content on the form, but that doesn't mean they're [in] any relation to one another.

--Thursday, March 10, 2011

Martha's Visit

Hi:

Martha was sitting in her chair twisted to one side. She
recognized me when I arrived and said that she felt fine. We
looked at the pop-ups from *The Little Prince*. She was able to read
the title to me but didn't show that much interest in the artwork.

I asked her if she would like to take a walk and she said no.

Her hair was cut short and her nails done. She looked
well-groomed.

At that time, we heard that Elizabeth Taylor had died today. I
asked her if she remembered her and liked her and she felt
positive about her. I was surprised to hear her ask, "what did she
die from?" I found out that she needs new pants and I tried to
get in touch with Jessica to see if she had purchased any since I
was close to JC Penny.

Spoke with E. Martha is stable. Feb. weight was 99.2; March's is
100.4.

[J]

Geriatric Care Manager

--Wednesday, March 23, 2011

King Lear Enters *The Little Prince*

It took me a long time to understand where he came from. King Lear, who asked so many questions, never seemed to hear the ones anyone else asked him. It was things he said quite at random that, bit by bit, explained everything. For instance, when he first caught sight of an airplane . . . he asked: "What's that thing over there?"

When told that the plane had fallen out of the sky, he asked what planet it was from.

"Of course," he said of the airplane, "that couldn't have brought anyone from very far . . . " And he fell into a reverie that lasted a long while. Then, taking a sheep out of his pocket, he plunged into contemplation of his treasure.

"You see me here, you gods a poor old man
As full of grief as age, wretched in both."

Something about his daughters was amiss but he would not draw them, nor even the castles they lived in. Another, I suspected, was houseless, wandering in a foreign (oh hard-to-spell!) land, exiled in more than word.

Lear liked the fox and the flower, but not the drunkard or the vain man who looked only and ever for approbation. He was vain, but he was also wise like the fox, lonely like the flower; his sense of place was a dark planet ("cerebral and dark," according to Netflix) on which he propped himself, bare and unforked. The drunkard and he could have talked story: *What is it about shame?* I'd have asked them, but neither drunk nor King could look beyond his bottle or word hoard. For a demented man, Lear sure seemed to carry around a lot of language. Paranoia's a fertile muse, but she also enters the drought years, rendering earth a cracked slab unbefitting a sovereign's looping locution. The master sees himself not so. "Here I stand your slave, / A poor, infirm, weak, and despised old man." He cannot count the stars, nor possess them, because he owes them his jangled moods, his love of piercing light, his debt to eyes that stay in his head. Sad news about his buddy Gloucester: the dead holes in his head,

the failed (if ably assisted) suicide, the inability to die even when
you or he ordain it. If to be sovereign means you get to choose,
then neither Lear nor his friend are so.

Enter the lamplighter. We more than suspect he's Edgar, playing
another's self (ragged beyond nounship), cold in the vog of a
 farther micro-planet. He cannot not light his lamp; his lamp
cannot not go out in the dark. Does Gloucester know this?
Gloucester cannot see, but Edgar is a more than able narrator.
"Father, for you are that, this planet's always on the limn of
darkness, save the man who cannot sleep for lighting the lamp."

Lear abhorred snakes, took refuge on mountaintops. He fancied
himself a thinker, unprovoked by daily needfulness. But the
snake kept slithering, and two daughters passed notes from desk
to desk, conspiring to wreak havoc. They were not flowers, at
least not those he wanted on his nightstand. So many thorns, as
if they needed protection from him. From him? He was just a
sojourner, a man who gave things away, making inheritance
while the sun shone on his white beard.

The railroad seemed one way out, though it hardly crossed the
planet borders without enormous slings. Bad engineering made
them slingshots, and trains transgressed the very skies, bearing
screaming children, angry commuters, releasing coal as acidic
rain in tunnels between stars. Don't tell the businessman; he
might become more generous with his constellations. Lear got
off at a distant station. No one worked in the building. A water
fountain had died long ago. The filing cabinets were full of old
teaching aids: How the Pilgrims Came to Plymouth Rock, The
Pioneers in Wagons, one with a picture of a sad chief. This did
not seem right, nor did it satisfy any thirst he had. He left the
station and its paper heaps and walked out into sand fields. A
pilot appeared, accoutered in cap and leather flying bag. He too
was lost.

There was a happy ending, at least for a time. Using dowsing
sticks, they found a spot, unmarked by stone or twig, dug until
they reached a vein of water. They drank from the same bucket,
sharing more than the cold water. But then the daughters came,
and their retinues, and their resentments, even the youngest
one's recovered love. There were swords and bitter words,

nothing water could wash away, not yet. Only the pilot escaped, muttering something about ripeness, about extremity, about trumpets. He took with him what memories there could be, left the stage a motley fool.

And no grown-up will ever understand such a thing. Never.

--April 25, 2011

Telephone Call

Is the heart of poetry a stillness? At the telephone's other end, *I'm here* and then she's not. *Just shut up and listen!* Jimmy Stewart yells on her television.

--Have you eaten, Mom?

--No.

--How's the weather?

–

--Are you there, Mom?

–

--I love you, Mom. I love you, Mom. I'll call back soon.

--[It's your daughter, Martha; she's on the phone.]

--Hello mom! How are you, mom? Did you just have lunch?

I hear you have a cold. Are you there, mom?

–

–

--[It's your daughter, Martha, she's on the phone. Say hello.]

--Hello. (breathy whisper)

--Hi mom, how are you? What have you been up to?

–

–

--[Hello.]

--I guess she's not up to talking today. I'll try back tomorrow, ok,
in case she's feeling more like it.

--OK, sorry. Good-bye.

--Tuesday, April 26, 2011

Mother's Day

--I'm looking for Martha Schultz on Country Lane.

--[Christine.] Martha, it's Susan. It's your daughter. On the phone. Say hello.

--H e l l o.

--Happy mother's day, mom!

--Thank you.

--How are you mom?

--

--Hope you're having a good day, mom.

--

--I'll call you back next week, mom.

--

--Love you, mom.

[Sounds from the television. Old movies. Laughter (from visitors?)]

--Sunday, May 8, 2011

Mom report / Susan Howe's *That This* / Albert Saijo's passing

Morning call from Arden Courts: mom has pneumonia. They've
done chest x-rays. She's very weak, "weaker than before."
[I'm having a hard time understanding the woman's accent on
the other end of the phone, so I ask her to repeat herself.] She
requests permission to call hospice. Yes, she would still be in
the same place, but might have a hospital bed. If she gets better,
they'll leave. I say yes, of course, thanks for calling. Yes.

When I look up "hospice" I get the word "palliative." Care that
makes patients more comfortable, lessens their suffering. Cloak.
Loose over-garment. Cloak and dagger. Superman. To cloak.
Conceal, cover over, hide. You cannot cover over pain, though
perhaps you can ease it.

Her death has been in my mind for days now. Bryant says we
had 2.5 inches of rain this morning between 5 and 8 a.m.
Rolling thunder, rain at times shearing toward the mountains,
plants fallen down on the lanai. When I heard that Mark's mother
was in ICU and then died, I worried that my mother does not die.
I cannot say that worry is easing, or that it's cloaked.

Say that her death is on or in my mind. What is death's shape, its
smell, what rent does it pay, or is there a mortgage, as it comes to
own us over time? Death is a resident; she lies on a bed and it is
to her that the cat comes. Cats know, you know. To reside is not
to abide, though it suggests a coming again (re-) to the activity
of being. Do not resuscitate. Do not force feed. Do not extend
beyond.

We own death (it is ours) for a time. We own it as concept, not as
fact. It is her death that is on my mind, though my death is there,
too. Hers and mine are relatives, but not the same. She gave birth
to mine, as I have adopted those of my children. It is still her
possession, even if she cannot understand it. But possession also
has an end. Not a possession to be bought or sold, but relinquished.
Into time, which is not one. I can say "her time has come," but that
is a double abstraction. She has her death, but not her time.

Radhika lies on the floor, reading *Diary of a Wimpy Kid*. She is singing or chanting, I cannot tell which, though I do distinguish the rain, water in the drain, thunder; I saw egrets on the lawn, white against dark green beneath gray. A day without horizon, thick. Kamehameha Highway is closed at Waikane. Bryant whistles: "waterfalls everywhere!" Every mountain fold water full.

That This. That is over there, this is over here. That happened; this is happening. Short vowels tucked into short words. They point. Which syllable is stronger, that one or this one? Is it that this? or that this? A line of egrets moves from this to that.

If I were writing the review of Susan Howe's book, as I'd planned, it would treat her invocation of "ancestors," those who "opened" Japan and traded with China. Or her sentence about Pearl Harbor and Hans Andersen. Her desire to be inside history, the discovery in grieving for her husband, Peter Hare, that she is relentlessly between things. Temporal tectonics.

"Somewhere I read that relations between sounds and objects, feelings and thoughts, develop by association; language attaches to and envelopes its referent without destroying or changing it-- the way a cobweb catches a fly" (13).

Language as cloak, what comes between the spider and her prey. Language as palliative, as nurse, as easing pain before an end. "More and more I have the sense of being present at a point of absence where crossing centuries may prove to be like crossing languages. Soundwaves. It's the difference between one stillness and another stillness. Even the 'invisible' scotch tape I recently used when composing 'Frolic Architecture' leaves traces on paper when I run each original sheet through the Canon copier" (31).

Howe moves from sound to sight, centuries to languages, scotch tape to the Canon copier. One of her favorite words is "hinge." A hinged picture squeaks.

"It could have been the instant of balance between silence, seeing, and saying; the moment before speech. Peirce would call this moment, secondness. Peter was returning to the common course of things--our world of signs" (35)

Howe's evocation of secondness, that instant between sound and silence, meaning and its release, comes in "Frolic Architecture," where material from the journals of Hannah Edwards Whitmore, sister to Jonathan Edwards, is cut and then spliced to the page with "invisible" tape. Among what's left of Hannah's words are markers of Howe's research: "1208 EP G 3 of 3 folders" (51). Secondness works in both directions, then, as a falling into silence and then a coming out of it, out from the aptly named "folder." Research is not rebirth, but.

Somewhere in the book's first section, "The Disappearance Approach," she writes about "cremains," or what is left of the body after cremation. I have a form on my other computer's desktop, filled out with instructions on what to do with my mother's cremains. The punster in me breaks out with, what we love best cremains. My mother's voice reminds me, they are the lowest form of humor.

The last word in "Frolic Architecture" is "sudden." As this word falls into that white page, it more resembles "sudder," then echoes "shudder." Sudden death, shudder. This is the opposite to my mother's death, which will not have been sudden. Her death will have an end, but it will not have been soon. That time will come.

I learned of Albert Saijo's death this morning. Saijo was a poet of the white spaces, especially toward the end when he refused to publish any of his poems. He was a beautiful man, and will be much missed by me and by my family. Rest well, Albert.

"But you're out. You went away and you came back. Now as you head back to civilization, you have a wildness in your heart that wasn't there before. You know you're going outback again."

--June 3, 2011

Note: Susan Howe, *That This*, New Directions, 2010. Albert Saijo, *The Backpacker*, San Francisco: 101 Productions, 1972, 1977.
102

The Difficulties of Long-distance Daughtering:
Updated Mom Report

Yesterday I wrote that my mother has pneumonia. Ah, the
misunderstandings of long distance daughtering--my mother
doesn't have pneumonia, after all. She's resting in bed, smiled at
the nurse (I was told on the phone), and then made it clear she
was through talking. That sounds like her.

From the social worker, yesterday:

Susan,

I am working with your mom until her new care manager
________ begins next week. I received a call from Arden Court
today and asked they contact you. The nurse reported to me that
your mom was started on an antibiotic for a cough this week.
They're concerned as she remains weak and her appetite has
decreased. They are thinking an evaluation by a hospice nurse
would be appropriate. Based on the information they told me, I
think this is appropriate. It would be an evaluation to determine
if she meets their criteria.

I don't know if Arden Court reached you and wanted to ensure
you are aware of their concern. I plan to visit your mom next
week to get an update on her status. Please contact me if you
have any questions. I will give you an update after I see her.

and today:

What I was told was that the xray was negative. I asked about
this because I was confused as to why she was started on an
antibiotic if the xray didn't show anything. The nurse explained
to me that she had a cough and has a history of pneumonia. It
then made sense that they were treating the symptoms and
attempting to prevent a pneumonia from developing. I'll double
check this. It appears there's a respiratory issue one way or
another. I am sorry that out of the blue I'm bringing you this
type of news. I'll let you know of any updates I receive as I plan
to follow up with the nurse over the weekend.

--Saturday, June 4, 2011

"Remember how to forget. No more."

A kind-sounding woman from Heartland Health Services calls to say they'll send two hospice nurses (one new, one experienced) to provide oxygen to mom later today. Am I familiar with hospice care? Have I known anyone in hospice care? Considering your mother's age (93) and condition, the doctor has requested it. They'll be calling later this week with reports on her condition. "Condition" reminds me of "situation." My father always said "situation" for "condition," for something about which he felt uncomfortable. You get rags lidat.

Funny you should ask. I was just looking in my on-line dictionary.

"Heartland Health is an integrated health delivery system." Their "outcomes are second to none." They have a standard of care that ends: "To help you die at home or in a setting of comfort and peace." When I said mom's been in the Alzheimer's home since late 2006, the kind-sounding woman said, "so that's home for her."

———————

This morning the nurse tells me she is trying to get oxygen for mom, but the hospice nurse didn't leave a call-back number, and she can't reach the main office. It's Sunday, which makes planning difficult.

"What made you want to look up *hospice*? Please tell us where you read or heard it (including the quote, if possible)."

When Amber puts me on hold, the usual musak starts up. "Be sure to come visit your family members," a voice-over tells me. Something about how important it is to visit. With strings.

I can't see mom, though I know she's in her room, pillows at her back, and she's not getting enough oxygen. "She's alert." There are numbers for breath, numbers for feeding, but I don't catch them as they fly in my ear.

The former neighbors say they'll pray for her.

The nurse says she'll call back when she reaches the hospice people.

"A facility or program designed to provide a caring environment for meeting the physical and emotional needs of the terminally ill" (*Merriam-Webster*). English-language learners get no euphemism: "a place that provides care for people who are dying." First known use, 1818.

"You're going away soon, aren't you?" someone asks me at a party yesterday. I bowled a spare. "Your daughter is strong," Kim tells me. "I like her," says Joy. Her ball halfway down the lane, Radhika turns and grins. Pins don't drop when she does. Earlier, she'd set up plastic water bottles in the living room and knocked them down with her soccer ball.

The central character in Embassytown is a simile. Her role is to liken one to another thing, render fact into fiction, truth into at least a partial lie. My mother is like a space traveler. She needs oxygen. Her narrow bed is like a rocket. Her level is at 20-something, not enough air. COPD makes it hard. There are pillows behind her. She smiled to Ellen & Steve when they stopped by. "She still understands something when I say your name," Ellen tells me on the phone. "At least that's what I choose to think."

The poet, Edwin Honig, died. A Facebook friend posts a clip from a short film about him. When asked what he might say to millions of people, if he had such an audience, he says (twice): "Remember how to forget. No more."

--Sunday, June 5, 2011

"Our spirit ever buoyant as we sink" (Albert Saijo)

Steve (friend on the inside) calls to ask if I want him to take the phone to my mother; he'll hold it to her ear. I say yes, I want that. So he introduces me to my mother; "Mahtha," he says in his Bronx accent, "this is your daughta, Susan; she wants to tawk to you." He tells me he's moving the phone to her ear, so I start delivering news to her. Radhika and I are cleaning house; Bryant and Sangha were out camping last night. Lightning, thunder. Hope she feels better. Respiratory problem--then it's Steve again to say my mother responds to my voice, that she's trying to talk back. There was no sound.

"Susan wants me to tell you that she loves you," says Steve to my mother. That's how it's done. We know the words and we say them for each other. It takes an Alzheimer's village to repeat these verbal saws because they're all we have. See saws. The back and forth, without the back--or is it forth?

As she loses speech, the blog goes out with more facts, fewer meditations. The hospice nurse who calls says there's a DNR for my mother, but is there a DNT? It takes a moment to remember that DNR stands for Do Not Resuscitate. No heroic measures. Should be NHM. DNT is about not transporting her from this place she knows to a hospital. I ask if I can call back; that is not a question I expected. I'm inclined to say yes, but need to talk to my husband. She says I might want to look into funeral homes. I don't remember paper work about that. Only about Georgetown Medical School. I will ask around, I tell her.

Alan Berliner, who made short films about Edwin Honig, who suffered from Alzheimer's, suddenly remembers why he called one box Picasso. That was the box containing film of his father making faces, slow faces, fast faces, taking off the glasses faces, the faces that reminded Berliner of Picasso, the painter Freud. But he had forgotten his own code. Until the film now brought it back. Take four. It was film, so there was no sound.

Honig says to remember how to forget. In another clip, he bangs on his chair, keeping rhythm as he arrives at a word that rhymes with jello. Don't you know it, he's a poet. Silliman wonders why facebook readers hit "like" at the announcement of Honig's death.

BODISATTVAHOOD IS A FUCKING JOB LIKE ANY OTHER.
Albert Saijo. So now let us be cheerful as we sink. Because there
won't be medicare or hospice care or heartland health or the car-
lyle group to get us through our Alzheimer's. The ship will sink
without our buddhas and our bodisattvas, or they will not have
insurance. We'll have to be in it for the poetry, the compassion,
the non-return on our investments, the lacks of prizes or recogni-
tions, the hard work for its own sake. Our friend has no space for
his wood carvings, so he carries them in his head. This is not a
solution. We suggest, considering the cost of living, that he start
cutting smaller pieces of wood, making micro sculptures. He
says woodworkers need their space. We feel silly for our practi-
calities. Know better.

I want to think that Saijo and my mother met in Italy in 1944.
I want to think those were his boots she kept in her closet, the
ones that fit. I want to think they ate the same bad food, saw
the same entertainers, drove the same trucks, watched Vesuvius
from the same hill on the same late afternoon. There are less
good reasons for relation than history, lots of them. But when
she got back from their war, Martha said she had no idea about
internment camps. Not the one Albert grew up in, not the others.
It wasn't in the newspapers.

I call the nurse back, say I've talked to my husband, yes we'd
like a DNT. She sounds relieved, talks about the significance of
staying at home. I wonder about transport. Bryant says the Boy
Scout skit had a Star Trek theme: "beam me up, Scottie," said
one boy, and another brought him a plank of wood. No, that's
teleporting. The trans- in transport does not take us anywhere.
That must be why it's beyond us.

Ben says Emerson's dementia did not emerge in his language,
but in his silences. The time before our lives was infinite, Howe
reminds us, and accepting that . . . we inherit ancestral quiet.
Dementia as return, not diminution. It's the round trip ticket we
got off the internet. Print out the receipt; evidence of your voy-
age will come later.

--June 6, 2011

Note: Albert Saijo, *Outspeaks: A Rhapsody*, Honolulu: Bamboo
Ridge Press, 1997.

106

"If increasing sadness": Muzak meditations

Arrived at the land of Muzak, not a destination really but a hold, a pause if not a rest. "When we listen to music," Susan Howe notes, "we are also listening to pauses called 'rests.' 'Rests' could be wishes that haven't yet betrayed themselves and can only be transferred evocatively" (TT 28). While Muzak means to offer calm, it cannot rest. Relentless Muzak. The tunes are not familiar, except as Alzheimer's music. The voice-overs aim to reassure the listener: your family member is very important to us. There is no sadness in the voice-over. When I reach Heartland Health, I hear the same muzak in my ear as at the Arden Courts number. "We're part of the same corporate food chain," I'm told by a hospice worker.

In the "Health and Safety Appendix" to the *Heartland Hospice Care Patient Information Handbook* that's sent me as a pdf, I find a chart. Three columns, from left: "Body System"; "Symptom"; "Comfort Measures."

Emma calls to say mom is "comfortable," and "in no pain." But she does not have funeral arrangements. She gives me two names. One is Money & King. May I laugh at the irony? I do not think the muzak would want me to.

Under "comfort measures" for "Symptom: Feeling sad," I find, listed after bullet points:

Offer gentle support
Allow discussion of feelings
Give medicine as ordered
Notify nurse if increasing sadness

What I'm told is that my mother speaks, but that she makes no sound. Ellen: "She 'mouthed' some words but I couldn't make out what she was saying. I told her that you send your love." Social worker: "When your mom was speaking to me this morning, she was not projecting much sound and it was primarily me under- standing the words she was mouthing to my questions."

Mouthing. When the mouth operates, but cannot project sound. The OED defines "mouthing" as

The action of mouth v. (in various senses); spec. the action of speaking in an empty, pompous, verbose, or foolish manner; an instance of this.

Merriam-Webster on-line defines it so, as well. The fourth definition works best: "to form soundlessly with the lips." The example has to do with a librarian. The librarian has volition; he knows he ought not to speak loudly, so he mouths his words. My mother tries to project sound, but none emerges. Another definition for the noun: "The entrance to an underground working from a mine shaft." To mine the mouth for words. To mine the mouth for words and come up without a seam, a vein, a breath. To go underground but not find the ground of saying. Form without content, and yet still content.

Muzak is mouthing's opposite. It's all sound, no meaning. No, that's not right. There's meaning, but meaning avoids the underground, the mouth, the vein, to pause in thought if not in time. "This is an odd mix of the practical with the metaphysical," I say to someone on the phone from hospice.

The blog is a mouth. It opens and closes with the other mouths. It is the entrance to a mine. It is sometimes thought to be pompous, bombastic, loose with the facts. It might be Muzak. But mine. Is meditation, is retrieval, is trying to make the sounds that mean. The Heartland handbook tells me, "You may be experiencing many emotions right now. Heartland Hospice is here to guide you on your journey." They mean my mother's journey, but it's mine. I am feeling pain. I am mouthing it. If you visit, you might hear it. In or out of the rests.

Why can't I remember the tune, the content of the voice-over? Why is there a cattle egret at the zoo, when I see three outside my window now, hunting roaches in the wet green grass? Why is memory what binds us together, like a simile, or "the cow stuff," as Sangha calls Elmer's? Why is ambition so predictable in its vehicles? Why does my chest quaver like a string? Why do doves coo, and mynas scream "cat!"?

I ask the social worker, the one who is working between the one who left and the one who has not yet started, if I should come to visit. It would have to be soon, as I'm in Scotland in July. I know this is a loaded question. [The cat comes out from under the bed; he will yell in a minute, as my door is closed. "Mom is busy," Bryant tells the kids.]

Susan,

Forgive my frankness.....if you are hoping to see your mom before anything happens then I think the trip in a couple of weeks is a good idea. With "seniors", conditions can change so quickly. She is weak. I've been surprised with other clients how quickly and suddenly their condition turned. I suggest you see her in a timely manner....just in case.

There are now six egrets on the field. The cat (a "senior") sits next to me, watches them, scratches his left ear with his back left leg. She might "turn" soon. A turn in a poem is when momentum breaks and the poet turns her wheel. Away from. Toward. "When we wander in circles / Driven by keen delusion / May the King of clear skies / Go before us, turning / The great wheel, and sounding the conch / on the path of radiant light / The way of all-embracing wisdom." This is where my eye falls when I write the word "turn." Sina sends her re-casting from the *Tibetan Book of the Dead* for Albert Saijo's passage. It's called "Fundamentals of Navigation."

Should I choose a funeral home by its website? Should I call and test their Muzak? Should I choose the home that uses metaphor? "We understand that family care extends beyond our front door." Ah, the "straits of the liminal." Or should I choose the home that uses a more literal approach? "Among the property's distinctive attributes are its front porch lined with rocking chairs."

The hospice nurse returns my call. Cannot tell if there's urgency or not. "Aspiration pneumonia," so it's pneumonia again. Oxygen mask, so she "obviously" can't say anything. Antibiotics. Not in distress. Comfortable. Will call back with any changes.

Another call. This time it's billing. She's going to send a form, but it's confusing, so she'll explain it to me. Medicare Part B, as in Boy. Three options. Advanced Beneficiary Notice. Medications may or may not be covered by Medicare Part B as in Boy or by the secondary insurer. "I presume you'd like me to choose the first option," I say, after she enumerates them. "I can't say anything more," she says.

"'Rests' could be wishes that haven't yet betrayed themselves," Susan Howe. Why the word "betray"? I know what mom would wish.

--June 6, 2011

Note: Susan Howe, *That This*. New Directions, 2010.

A Formal Feeling Comes; or, Just Forms

I am aware of the prognosis of my illness and I understand that
treatment is palliative rather than curative. I consent to the
management of the symptoms of my disease as prescribed by
my Attending Physician and/or the Hospice Medical Director.
My family and I will help to develop and will participate in a
plan of care based on our special needs.

[Virginia Dept. of Medical Assistance Services, Request for Hospice
Benefits form]

How will my body be received once it arrives at Georgetown?
Very special care will be given to your very special gift. You can
be assured that your remains will always be treated respectfully,
carefully, and sensitively. The doctors, students and healthcare
professionals here are mindful of your serious and generous
intention to enhance their opportunity to study human anatomy.
They are aware of their debt to you for offering them such a
priceless source of learning. [Georgetown University School of
Medicine, "Information on Bequeathal"]

In accepting these services, which are more comprehensive than
regular Medicaid benefits, I waive my right to regular Medicaid
services that are duplicative of services required to be provided
by the Hospice except for payment to my Attending Physician or
treatment for medical conditions unrelated to my terminal illness
. . . I may be responsible for hospice charges if I become ineligible
for Medicaid services. [VA Dept.]

I understand that unless the donor has indicated her/his preference,
which is binding, Georgetown will not share the use of a cadaver
with another Medical School without the permission of the Next of
Kin. [Georgetown]

Mercy wanders in the desert for 40 days and 40 nights. She
climbs to the top of a mountain, one of the Old Woman
Mountains. She sits down, filthy and hungered. *Who.*
Why aren't you floating? I have to do this this way.

[Alice Notley, *Culture of One]*

I understand that I may be billed for co-payments and deduct-
ibles required by my medical insurance. I understand that I am
responsible for notifying Heartland immediately of any change
in my insurance coverage and that I am responsible for any
charges not paid by my insurance carrier resulting from my
failure to do so in a timely manner. [ADMISSION AGREEMENT:
Election of Hospice Benefit and Consent to Treat]

Dear Dr. Braddock:

If you die in your sleep do you know you are dead? Your
clinically precise word order is a failure of dream-work. It gives
an effect of harmless vacancy. Why this violent tearing away?

Sincerely,

[Susan Howe, *That This*]

EXCLUSIONARY CRITERIA
(Revised from *"Donating Your Body to Science"*)
7. The donor is in fetal position or has contracted limbs.
Rationale: *The body must lay flat on a table in order to be placed in
our storage area.*

————————

May the elements of the earth not rise up against us or the elements
of forms, containers, urns, bearers of ash. My son's teachers say
his prosody is good when he reads. He scans. I scan form after
form, email, pdf, fax, fail. Repeat. I understand the progress of
my treatment, where I am my mother. I do not sign for--but as--
her.

My sister-in-law tells me about a book in which the inside is
larger than the outside of a house. The house of my mother's
body still contains her. Not the body a "memory table" can
organize, but one on which photographs are set beside the white
out. Each visitor must dip his brush into the white substance and
cover over a part of her face, her arms, her legs, her breasts, the
cigarette she held up in the 1950s black and white snapshot.

Her body is an urn. Ern Malley was a fake. Poet of air, not the
dump. Culture of one, where one is multiples of one. He was
two men, but a third poet. Why do we say a dog has a good
"personality"? The neighbor who walked Murphy died; I knew
his widow by the dog she walked. She is she because his little
dog loves her. I call Murphy's Funeral Home to make back-up
plans, just in case mom's body is "excluded." It's a family-run
business. There are the Murphy's on their website, all eight of
them, looking out. It was Martha J. Keefe, because the "O" had
been too Irish. Whited out. Half the women in Cork looked like
her.

I can't remember why I wanted to make a codex.
Marie doesn't know the word "codex." But she tries not
to remember, by making what she makes containing
all her memories and yours, o garbagers

[Alice Notley]

Random access memory. Trunk of a tree or block of wood. The
plank in reason. Rationales for "exclusionary criteria": as if fact
mitigates fact. If your body is obese, it will not fit in our storage
area. Or: "the anatomical relations are altered." No alteration
where alteration found. Donne was a nasty poet, Ben notes.
Ambition is as ambition does. Has nothing to do with flies, but
with aggression. "The point is not to suppress your anger, but to
watch it and let it go," writes The Motocycliste on Daily Kos.

I am short with family, short with friends, short with cat, short
with dogs, short with newspaper commenters, short with
people on the phone. I am short. My mother is short, as was
my father. Shortness runs in the biological family. My mother's
body, stepping into the tub, taught me what a woman's body
is. Pubic hair red, her head of hair brown. (Born a red-head, her
hair color changed within days.) It is now mapped otherwise.
Choose satellite or map, or the hybrid that offers pegs & pins on
photographs of actual streets. They will try not to use IVs, as that
might exclude her body from "donation to science."

In Notley's book, Marie's shack gets burned down, and again.
Her dog is killed by mean girls. My mother's mother put her dog
to sleep when she was away. My mother's body is a house that

will be burned. Her cremains revert to Next of Kin, where Next of Kin is I who sign the forms as her.

It means that I make perfect sense.

[Notley]

The the. That this. Here, thereafter.

--Thursday, June 9, 2011

Note: Alice Notley, *Culture of One*. Penguin Books, 2011.

Dying: A Self-Help Manual

Mr. Murphy was dying. Mrs. Murphy came to visit. For three days they talked & wept. Sister Brigid wondered if she should intervene. But on the fourth day, Mr. and Mrs. Murphy laughed. Sister Brigid asked Mrs. Murphy what had happened. Mrs. Murphy told her they had spent those days sharing memories of their 40 years together. "This story," the Rinpoche writes, "shows to me the importance of telling people early that they are going to die, and also the great advantage of facing squarely the pain of loss" (Sogyal, 179).

Books about dying are books about talking. They advise the dying to talk, and the living to talk, the dying to talk to the living and the living to the dying, and they talk about all of this. We ease our fears by talking; we clear our psychic inventories by talking; we are cured through our communicative powers. "When I hold her hand," Christine said this morning, "she rubs her thumb back and forth on it, like she did when I walked her to the community center." At meals, I remember, she moved her thumb back and forth over her own other hand.

"Talking about dying is very difficult," David Kuhl writes. "We are afraid that talking about death beckons it" (xv). I say my mother is in hospice, and what I hear back most often is quiet.

--She's weak, she's very weak. Closes her mouth when she doesn't want to eat. We bring her soft foods, puddings, oatmeal, jello. Not doing well on Ensure. Likes the cranberry. She closes her mouth sometimes when she doesn't want us to feed her.

--Did you tell her I'm coming? Next Thursday.
--Yes, oh yes, and I'm going to keep telling her.

Like the first rush of a martini, like the moment meditation reaches the top of the skull, like the time you notice leaves in the air between your eyes and the Ko`olau, like the inside of a house that is suddenly larger than its exterior, like a meadow that stretches like toffee, like a simile strained to the point of rupture, like an active alert patience, grieving.

An impossibly synchronous annoyance. Do not play your video game so loudly. Do not leave your trash in the living room. Do not tease me. Do not stop packing for your camping trip. Do not look at me that way. Do not pass me the phone. Do not treat me like this is an ordinary day. Don't you understand!?

"Connect by talking. Connect by listening. Connect by encouraging memories" (Miller).

I talk to the nurse at Arden Courts. I talk to the nurse at Heartland Hospice. I email the social worker from the care-management agency. I talk to the receptionist. I talk to the man at Murphy's Funeral Home. I email my lawyer. I email the hospice people about Medicare forms, requests to treat forms, requests not to treat too much forms. I send attachments about the body being given to science. I talk again to all of the above.

Bryant and Sangha are on Kaua`i, camping. If they are near a cell tower, they will call. Bryant did not call last night; he has not called this morning.

The books do not tell me how to connect without talk, without sound, without memories. The books do not tell me what it means to grieve one-sidedly. The books do not tell me this isn't so, that there are as many sides as during meditation--no sides at all. The books keep talking at me. I am at a lecture on grieving and there are five stages to learn for the exam. This will be the most difficult exam you will ever take, I'm told. The results will be scientific, as the form is multiple-choice. You will find your-self a) calm; b) angry, or c) watching a lot of baseball on your computer. The Greek word is a) thanatos, or b) minotaur. Be sure to use a number two pencil and press with confidence.

Which of the following statements is most helpful to the loved ones of a dying family member?

1) DO NOT BE SO NEGATIVE.
2) You are so much on my mind right now.
Word problem: You are on an ocean liner looking in at a dock of faces looking out. There is the space between you, which breathes. If you look at the water's surface, you see flying fish,

birds, whitecaps. (The telephone lines at Souza Dairy field yesterday rippled with light, as if there were abacus beads floating back and forth between old wooden poles.) A canoe sets out from the dock, but it does not have the ocean liner's horsepower (sic). Someone is paddling toward the ocean liner as quickly as she can, left hand at the top, at the bottom, right. Will she get there in time? What equation do you plan to use in your calculations? (Be sure to record the process of your work, as well as your final results on the test paper.)

May the Queens of space and hosts
Of angels come behind us, circling
To cover our backs
And together deliver us
From the dreadful
Straits of the liminal, and carry us
To the shores of freedom. [Fundamentals]

I always thought it would be wonderful to be reborn as a seagull, my mother said, until I realized that they live on garbage.

--Friday, June 10, 2011

Notes:

David Kuhl, M.D., *What Dying People Want: Practical Wisdom for the End of Life.* (NY: PublicAffairs, 2002). This book belonged to Scott Swaner, a Tinfish translator, and was sent to me by his sister, Sheri, after he died. Thank you, Sheri.

James Miller, "Ideas for a Time When Someone You Love is Dying," http://angel-on-my-shoulder.com/ideas.html

Sogyal Rinpoche, *The Tibetan Book of Living and Dying.* San Francisco: HarperSanFrancisco, 1994.

Caroline Sinavaiana's version of "Fundamentals of Navigation" from *The Tibetan Book of the Dead.*

Thank you to Mark Scroggins for offering the right answer above.

Shatner Chatter: Or, Post-Human Travel Plans

Last night:

Hi Susan,

*Thanks for your email. Unfortunately, it does seem like your mom is
getting weaker. I'm so sorry. Please keep us posted with regard to your
travel plans. Also, if you need us for anything, please don't hesitate to
give us a call. We'll be around all weekend (in and out).*
Take care.
Love,
Ellen

This a.m.: "Secure" on the Arden Courts waiting message sounds
at first like "cure."

--She ate 25% of her breakfast. We couldn't get her in a wheel-
chair to go to the community room. She's very weak. [I ask.] Yes,
come earlier.

Nurse says the same thing.

Got tickets for Thursday arrival through priceline.com. Plane
and rental car for less than a round-trip ticket. I booked the hotel
on the wrong night. Can't ever remember that red-eyes take up
the night. I call priceline, get William Shatner, a phone tree, no
persons. I look at united.com, but there are no phone numbers.
There is no phone number for United Airlines in either of my
Honolulu telephone books. They merged, so I call Continental,
get Daphne. Daphne looks up my reservation, says United owns
it, gives me their number. Phone tree. I speak loudly--too loudly
--to the automated voice. I get a person. I tell him how grateful I
am to have a human being, and he thanks me. It's then I realize
that he sounds automated. He is sorry to hear about my mother,
but he can't do anything, because I made the plans without an
agent. I call priceline again, more Shatner, no human being.

I can get a one way ticket to DC, which is not Baltimore, where I
will have a rental car on Thursday, the day after my hotel
reservation begins in Fairfax, and where I'll return from. I can get
a one way ticket to Baltimore, but it's crazy. I will get the ticket
to National. I will beg them to change my rental car reservation
and they will tell me they cannot. It's not them, it's priceline, and
I refuse to talk to William Shatner any more. He can beam me
nowhere.

I call the cousin down the street. I will leave Radhika with them
tomorrow. They can pick up Bryant and Sangha in the evening
from Kaua`i. Or I can leave the car and let them know where it is
at the airport and they can tell Bryant when he arrives. Bryant
cannot be reached. He is on High Adventure with the Boy Scouts.

I am on High Adventure with priceline.com. I hit the purchase
button. The screen tells me they are negotiating deals. Little dots
flash at me. Birds on a wire. William Shatner is there, one fist
jabbing the air toward me, the other held back. He is shadow-
boxing, as am I. They have made me a good deal. Too bad it's
the second deal I've made this week. Two good deals do not one
make.

My mother broke her pelvis a couple of months before our
wedding. She canceled her flight reservations. "I got my money
back!" she told me on the phone. She was well by the time we
married. She would not want me spending her money this way.

I call Arden Courts back, say I'm coming Monday, please keep
her going until then. "We're trying," says the caregiver.

--Saturday, June 11, 2011

Like a Walking Meditation Without the Walk: Travel Day 1

On the television this morning, auto racing (delayed for rain in Montreal) & motorcycle racing. Engines whine. The tracks are circles we cannot trace. The man who taught us to make fish hooks has his students draw. Unless you see the form in your mind, you cannot make the makau, he says. Ernesto Pujol walks toward me at the gallery cafe; I know him from his videos, photographs, I know him from his walking meditations. *I heard about you from a hotel clerk in Lawrence, Kansas*, I say. That was his student in Utah. (The link is an orphan.) I do not say that I love Albert Pujols, that his slump is over, that he shaved, that he too walks a lot.

A mode of art that is not power, but offers us a model. When I watch you walk, I see feet, legs, knees, hands, narrow sideburns. Robes make it harder to see the legs, the knees, though they make the body whole. Anne says when we die, she likes to think we become one with ourselves. Without the seams. Unseamly. Unseemly blog, you carry me forward to your own end. Shall I grieve for you, too? This odd & backwards walk, like memory but without the memory. (They hand out flash drives like candy these days.)

Mode, model, make. My Versa followed by a white hearse yesterday. Pick-up truck whose license read "Viet 67." Combat plates.

The epiphany for me is in the first 10 minutes or so about meeting form with formlessness as the way to neutralize violence. I cannot say that death is a form, but it is not violence now. Is the meeting of. Dogen: "to accept a body and give up a body is an act of generosity." To speak of death is not violence. To write the blog is not violence. To walk is to meet formlessness with two feet, awkward prosody.

"She floats," the soccer moms say. "Did you see that?!" Floakers. There are characters in *Embassytown* who sound out a language, but cannot speak it. They say it to each other as a French speaker speaks English to another Frenchman who speaks English in return. The way we stuttered French on the buses, children staring

at us with dilated eyes. But when they speak to a native, none
understands sound as meaning. It's a mother tongue that cannot
be transferred. She is your only mother, the one who is dying
like a language, steady distress of verbs & nouns breaking into
pieces. But this is not violence. Is mending. Words falling petal-
wards into color, fabric--out of lamination and into air. Lamentation,
heir.

Paul writes to say he'll publish *Memory Cards*. His father was
in hospice for four 1/2 years. No typo where none intended.
Deck of cards. House of cards. Even in board games, my mother
refused to gamble or borrow money. Would not mortgage Board-
walk, would not collect $200, would not obey the little yellow
cards.

Sina is meeting me at the airport with the *Tibetan Book of the Dead*.
Translated so many times, there's more than one page on Amazon.
It's Thurman, the one whose daughter acts. That's the one to read.
On the plane. Honolulu to Somewhere, Somewhere to Dallas,
Dallas to Washington, DC. Your car will be in Baltimore on
Thursday. Synchronicities happen, but not through priceline. I
want a fucking person on the goddamn phone.

Martha is "the same." She has not eaten today. It took three tries
to get a voice on Country Lane. This voice is softer than usual.
She's having a hard time swallowing. See you tomorrow. Thank
you for taking care of her.

When *see you tomorrow* is an act of faith. When an act of faith is
an entirely present thing. Like the row of raindrops under the
dark brown rail on the lanai. When an act of faith is not simile, or
simulacrum. Fulcrum. Fullness. Air

With deep thanks to Norman Fischer & Caroline Sinavaiana,
whose words are appropriate(d) here, and to Paul Naylor for his
support over many years.

--Sunday, June 12, 2011

A death in the family

Martha Jean Keefe Schultz, October 25, 1917-June 14, 2011

After the Hyphen

An hour's sleep & then my thumb pulls the peel off a ball of
light.

Panic attack without panic. Hours & days before the end, I read
in the brochure that hospice left, the dying person experiences
surges of energy. I saw none in her, but now in me a rivered
string of lights is coming down the street, house by house, as it
did after a power outage in what, 1968?

An hour before she died, her breath kept catching, as if her body
forgot intake out take intake & out. Then habit returned effort to
her open mouth.

Dying is a verb.

Tia wanders in and out of this. She was my mother's neighbor
on Country Lane, hair dyed black, jacket checked black & white,
slacks black, arthritic fingers painted off-red. What's going on,
she asked at Martha's door, yesterday, which is now the day
before. My mother's sleeping, I said. She'll be ok. No, she's not,
Tia replied, reaching a hand out to mom's forehead, shaking it
back and forth. Tried to pour water into mom's mouth before I
said no, they did that with the sponge.

After mom died at 6 pm, Esther teased Roland that he'd need a
new girlfriend. He was the one who, when he told my mother to
get up for dinner, she did. Esther got her elbow in the ribs. Not
Roland, the tall man. She always did like men, I said. Tia, standing
next to Esther, called out, Yes she did!

Ellen took me home with her and Steve. They & Max asked
about my father. I offered history: Michigan farm, auto plant,
air force, IBM, Western Union. Ellen said, Jerry Lawler. Jerry
Lawler! My father's Irish friend, office roommate of Col. Dudley
Stevenson, Tuskegee airman. Steve called Jerry; we explained the
coincidence. He darted off to find a letter. Please, do you mind?
I'm looking. *Dear Jerry, the letter read. My father's voice, Irished.
Jerry, you never put yourself above others, gave credit to them & did
not take it. The experience of an Irish immigrant. Martha & Susan join
me in wishing you a long & enjoyable retirement.*

Ellen's family in the concentration camps. Mom there when Dachau was liberated. Her memory was stronger than the first impression. Men in striped pajamas making shelters out of anything they could find.

C & Roland wash mom's body. Suddenly, from C's phone, the voice of a child singing in Tagalog. *My niece, she's three years old.* The only Tagalog she knows is what she sings.

The day I left Hawai'i I took my usual bike ride. Was side-swiped by a silver pickup truck that didn't stop. Knocked to the asphalt of Kam Highway near the old Pineapple Hut. As I tried the bike, a man called out from down the road, asking if I needed a ride. Should have gotten the plate number, he said. He was a wind-mill worker from Pahala, living in Hau'ula, who picked up my bike, put it in his truck, drove me home. I tended to the bleeding elbows, later found a deep bruise on my right hip. Only when I arrived in Virginia did I feel the heart bruise, blue circle embedded near the center of my left breast.

Roland dressed mom in navy blue pants, & a blue & white striped shirt. When I came back to walk her to the black SUV with flashing lights (give my body to science, she always said, and we did), a man in sun glasses attached a tag to her big marbled toe. Check the spelling, he said. Esther had already witnessed the act.

Om mane padme hung.

--June 14, 2011

'The key is in the sunlight at the window in the bars the key is in the sunlight"

--Your mother was in the common room after dinner on Tuesday, wasn't she? I was surprised to see her there, says the new resident's relative. The new resident is Io, who screamed help! the day my mother died.

--No, she died at 6 p.m. She couldn't move.

--My mother always asked why her husband never visited after he died. She had psychic powers. She worked on them. I have them, too, but I'm scared to push; you can get to the dark side so quickly. Your mom was sitting in that chair. She would usually greet me, if only with her eyes. But this time there was no response.

--I don't usually tell people, she adds, so they don't think I'm loony.

--I left deliberately, says the gentlest caregiver. I pray for you, you know. You're always here alone. Be strong. Yes, I heard the story from Roland about your father's voice. He told me.

The lawyer says it doesn't matter about the will if you're an only child. There's some hierarchy, her assistant tells me, before she arrives. Marriage, children, unless you remarry and there are more children, or earlier ones. I get lost in the possibles.

--No, there's no funeral, I tell the cook, who asks about a *bewing*. She gave her body to science, and then I'll get the ashes. Never wanted a funeral anyway.

--I can see that! I'd love to have my remains spread in the ocean waters.

--Let me do it for you. We have lots of ocean.

She will rest in peace, the old neighbor writes from his Android. Everything an ad, an alert, a pointer toward. The lawyer says her niece, the one going to Vandy, loves Walmart. Let me tell you, she said to her niece. How you spend your money.

I always get lost in Arlington. I plot out my route, and I follow it.
Up to a point. The Washington Monument appears and it's not
what I want. Circle back, find the lawyer. *Are you lost, too?* asks
Sylvia, when I say good-bye to her. She carries two purses, full of
apples, oranges. No, not this time, I say.

I say good-bye to Mrs. Lee, to whom I gave mom's orange dog,
the one with alien eyes. I kept the rabbit she held when she
died. Mrs. Lee looks at me and laughs. I say good-bye again. She
laughs.

I say good-bye to Florence, the woman who talks, even if
sentences are not plotted against a graph of sense. I'm tired, she
tells me. So *droopy*. She was fighting the caregivers the other day,
didn't want the girls to have to help her in the bathroom. Her
white narrow-cabled sweater has a stain on the front, like my
mom's when I left it in her room to be given away.

I thank Tia for her kindness. She says her daughter brought her
here, holds out her hand, as if her daughter were seven or eight
years old. She turns the wrong way. Gloria says they haven't
served lunch. Only a cracker. Only cheese and a cracker. She's
hungry. Walks to the clock in the right corridor, where I've led
them. Two hours until they feed us!

Meera practices telling time over dinner, looks at the hands, the
every other number on her father's watch. Her brother walks
us through his trilogy. Templars, an Academy, children being
misused to violent purpose. He and a friend infiltrating to save
them. A hole in the wall that's meant to look like a hole in the
wall, though it isn't.

I say good-bye to them, too. There's no reason to return, if you
take family as the baseline, "blood relation" as trump card,
though blood thins. *That's odd, her pulse is normal, just weak,* said
the nurse, a minute before mom passed.

She fought so hard to stay alive. It was time, Lena tells me.
Amazing how they know when it's time to die, says Emma.
Shook her head. No food. No more. Willed it.

"Strange to think of you, gone without corsets & eyes, while I walk on the pavement of Greenwich Village."

Whom to believe, the one who saw her struggle to live, or the one who saw her choose her exit? She was in her bed when she was in the chair after dinner. She was a ball of light in my hotel room. She was whatever was intended.

———

Two lines of poetry from Allen Ginsberg's *Kaddish and Related Poems* (1959-1960) from his *Collected Poems*.

Thank you to Josh & Gini, Sam & Meera, to Kyle, Pia, & Esben, & to Steve, Ellen & Max for three mind-lifting evenings of good & loving company this week. To Jerry, who gave me back my father's voice so soon after my mother died. To Elizabeth Wildhack, Esq. & the adroit accountant, Arlene Millican. And to everyone who called, wrote, facebooked, emailed, took time. Thank you to the caregivers, the hospice workers, the doctor (Hermes!) who arrived at mom's door the very moment she died, the compassionate people who populate this world that I leave, for now, & to which return is required, but not always to be feared.

--June 17, 2011

A shadow-talk with Roland Barthes on mourning

RB's mother died 10/25/1977, which was my mother's 60th birthday. I found his mourning diary at Bridge Street Books today. Many entries do not resonate for me, but some do profoundly. He wrote his notes on index cards; they were only published in 2009 in France, and in 2010 in the US. I want to talk back to him (the belated talking to, when one party is unable to speak in the present) about many of his notes.

So, RB like this, *SMS like this*. We're at a cafe somewhere, calling and responding.

--I don't want to talk about it, for fear of making literature out of it--or without being sure of not doing so--although as a matter of fact literature originates within these truths. 10/31

The strange phrase here is "without being sure of not doing so," even more so because the full sentence turns on the pivot between a fear of literature and acknowledgment that this is what it's made of. Why the fear of literature in the face of death? Or is it the too-sudden emergence of literature, before the mourning period makes it somehow appropriate? When I began my blog, I had no idea it would record her death in some near-present tense; had I thought toward the moment . . .

--A strange new acuity, seeing (in the street) people's ugliness or their beauty. 10/31

This rhymes with my experience, though usually without the suffix of "ugliness or beauty." I simply notice them more, when I see something other than my thoughts--not distractions, except when I'm driving (or riding my bike). Altered states are not states so much as wobbles, the inside of a balloon as the air comes in and then exits, quickly. Pfffft.

--What's remarkable about these notes is a devastated subject being the victim of presence of mind. 11/2

Again, I don't think the word "victim" sings to me, but the rest of the sentence does. During her last hour, her hand seemed to be melting, mottles into skin, skin into nails, fingers into fingers. When my urgency was not to save her, but to send her on as well as I could.

--henceforth and forever I am my own mother. 11/4 (which was the day of my father's death in 1992)

And henceforth this writing about my mother will be writing about me. And that is some of what makes me feel nervous, awkward. Until now, I was not the story, the story was my mother's dementia, that of her colleagues at the Alzheimer's home, the story of care, of pain, of memory jostled, necessary, in the face of forgetfulness. To what extent can writing about grief be about the person who is gone? Or are we now left with ourselves as subject, object, verb? During dementia, there were losses but there was not Loss. Grief is official now. But whose is it? Hers, mine, that of the cloud in which our information is stored?

--Struck by the abstract nature of absence . . . Which allows me to understand abstraction somewhat better; it is absence and pain, the pain of absence--perhaps therefore love? 11/10

Abstraction used to feel like a place of refuge. Like the place you could go when the kapu was broken, and you'd be safe. Now it is not only a spirit (instead of material person) but a spirit that is moving away. Not public transport, nor private, but transport nonetheless, and not (necessarily) solitary. I must follow the track of the Tibetan Book. I lost it on Tuesday. Bard, bardo. A soul in search of her next incarnation. One hopes she's not in northern Virginia's traffic pattern, blocked arteries on a Saturday afternoon.

--Mourning: a cruel country where I am no longer afraid. 11/17

The mind softens, the Buddhists say. Every blow makes us more pliable, more liable to adjust, not to duck but to face forward, absorb punishment as something more loving than that. When Barthes writes of not being afraid, he means that he has suffered until he knows how. It's not alleviation of suffering, at least not at first, but the promise it will at once go and be our guide. In the middle of the woods and all that.

and especially:

--[Status confusion]. For months, I have been her mother. It is as if I had lost my daughter (a greater grief than that? It had never occurred to me.) 11/19

*She was neither mother nor daughter at the end. I have a daughter,
who is not powerless, says what she means to say. But she was not my
mother, either, except as the living memory of her. The body is memory,
even after the mind checks out (extended stay is not home). She was like
the spirit in Beloved, at once a person and a ghost. But those who stop
visiting Alzheimer's patients think ghost, not person. Person is there to
be seen.*

--What I find utterly terrifying is mourning's discontinuous
character.

*In my stupor today I watched golf on television. There is a new golfer;
he's Irish. He was wearing a baby blue shirt, an ad on his white cap.
But to watch golf is not to know where you are in time or place. It's
not on a field you can take in, the players all in the same space, time.
Instead, the game discontinues, from hole to hole, frontwards and then
back. It's grief without the affect, merely the motion of grieving, the
arcs that are not yet circles, the holes that have not yet been filled with
flags (mom died on Flag Day at the home). It's important to die at
home, they told me.*

After that point, Barthes' entries replay themselves, a circling
that fails--that does not try--to close. Love for mother becomes
love for grieving over her (perhaps). He's not reached mourning;
he's at the many stations of melancholia. At some point in late
1978, when he was still taking these notes, I attended one of his
talks at the Sorbonne. I remember nothing of it, save a solitary
man sitting in front of a semi-circle of seats, his audience rapt in
its devotion.

--Saturday, June 18, 2011

Note: Roland Barthes, *Mourning Diary*, translated by Richard
Howard. NY: Hill & Wang, 2010.

The contents of my mother's drawer

At the end of her life, my mother had hardly any possessions
--some clothes, an ancient television, a couple of pieces of furniture
(were those even hers?). But she did have the contents of a bed-
side drawer, where I found all of these items except a photo of my
dad, which was perched on a ledge above her. It appeared to have
been folded and injured, probably by her: one of her neighbors is
infamous for destroying family photos unless they're contained in
the sealed box outside her door. There are photos we sent her of
the kids; a Ph.D. graduation photo; some birthday cards, the most
recent of which was 2007 or so; there are lyrics to religious songs,
including "Mansion Just Over the Hilltop," which begins: "I'm
satisfied with just a cottage below, / A little silver and a little gold;
/ But in that city where the ransomed will shine, / I want a gold
one that's silver lined." Finally, there's a small ripped out section
of a novel that belonged to another resident, namely *Hobgoblin*, by
John Coyne. (This resident turns out to be one of the lovebirds.) The
first page of this copy, which is page 277 of the book, has quite a sex
scene on it; at the bottom, etched into the page from an earlier one,
can be found seven question marks.

--Monday, June 20, 2011

Elegy

Dementia Blog began August 1, 2006 with this:

--Shown a photograph of herself and Sangha (2 or 3 years ago), she doesn't recognize herself. That's my mother, she says.

It has ended with the contents of her drawer at Arden Courts of Fair Oaks in Fairfax, mainly photographs she could not identify by name, place, or time. There were lyrics to songs she did not sing, part of a novel she doubtless did not read.

————

My mother's dementia preceded the blog, and my memories of her will postdate it. But the blog was a place of paradoxes, an obsessively-kept record that memorialized her forgetting.

What it did not call forth was a woman who told wonderful stories about her adventures in North Africa and Europe during WWII, who married late, who became a mother later than that, tried hard not to replicate the patterns of her own growing up (succeeding, failing).

It did not offer evidence of her wry wit, her sarcasm ("if this plane goes down, all the fish in the sea will be drunk," she said before one trans-Atlantic flight; "you'd have to be awfully sober to find your house in this neighborhood," she said of a suburban cookie-cutter community).

It did not tell the story of her childhood in an alcoholic family (hence the jokes).

It did not tell of her work for the rich old woman in Meadville, Pennsylvania, Mrs. Kidder, or of the black man named Lincoln who sang about the caged bird.

It did not tell of her M.A. in Speech and Drama from the University of Iowa ("Oh, I do a little Speech," she would tell people, lest they think her one of *those* students).

It did not tell of her work at Grinnell College for a stern older
dean, where she hid students' illegal animals--pig, chicken--in a
basement until they all got busted. It did not tell of her time at
Northern Michigan, where the president of the college had hair
dryers installed in the women's bathroom six feet off the ground,
where only he could use them.

It did not tell of her adventures in north Africa, where she
worked for the Red Cross and ducked in a ditch to avoid a
bombing raid, where she saw a dead body stuffed in a trash can
in Algiers.

It did not tell how she invaded Italy with the US Army (in her
function as administrator of entertainment to US troops), how
she witnessed battles, met men who never came back from their
own bombing raids, got a pair of small combat boots from one of
the "Neecy boys" of the 442nd.

It did not tell of the time she was driving a truck—later she
would say, you know I drove a truck in the War—and thought
she'd run over a child.

It did not tell of her experience of the Battle of the Bulge, or of
how she was at Dachau when it was liberated, of how it took her
several days to even know what she had seen--all the bodies on
the train cars, bodies everywhere, men in pajamas making shelters
for themselves out of anything they found around them.

It did not tell of how she chanted "war is hell" the one time (she
says) she got drunk, in Bad Neuheim, Germany, where she told
them either to fix her dripping toilet or take it away, so they
took it away, or of how she danced naked in the moonlight in
north Africa after drinking spiked wine, had to be restrained by
several grown men.

It did not tell of the pilot she knew whose life was changed when
he witnessed a little girl running in terror from bombs, or the
pilot who threatened never to come back from his mission if his
girlfriend refused to marry him, and she did, and he did not.

It did not tell of how a soldier greeted her every day with "when will you marry me?" til she got the chaplain to come along; when the soldier asked next, she said, "how about now?" and that was the end of that. It did not tell how she almost told stories about her friends' abortions.

It did not tell of how she met my father and pretty much tackled him, of how a psychic had told her years before who he would be, or of the hearts she broke before she met him.

It did not tell of the rainbow she saw as she drove over the Scottish border once, which made her happy she did not have a camera because then she could really see it, the green grass and the sheep.

It did not tell of how she asked someone to show her the Bastille and he pointed to the street, nor did it tell how someone asked her directions and she answered, laboriously, in French, only to realize they had asked her in English.

It did not tell how fierce a mother she was, protective and sometimes vicious.

It did not tell how she would get angry and withdraw, sometimes for days, refusing to speak to her daughter, or of how she would mysteriously reappear, softening over hours.

It did not tell how that happened at Lenin's Tomb in 1981.

It did not tell of how we would sometimes lie in bed and giggle hysterically.

It did not tell of the pianist she'd seen at a concert once with enormous sleeves, who swoooped and swoooped over the keys like a huge bird.

It did not tell how she would eavesdrop on conversations and then repeat them better than they'd happened, or how she met a Swiss woman in a cafe in Basel (?) and, without any shared language, learned the story of the woman's son.

It did not tell how she had survived amoebic dysentery in north
Africa only after a doctor suggested she use mineral oil, or how
she demanded mineral oil when she got sick on a trip in Norway.

It did not tell how she communicated her need for tissues by
vividly pretending to blow her nose outside a shop.

It did not tell how she settled in to suburban life, filling her
houses with bad furniture and art.

It did not tell how she told me to listen when Martin Luther King
came on the large wooden radio because he used English so well.

It did not tell how she would recite part of "Captain, My Captain"
or the poem about being master of your fate and captain, as if it
were possible.

It did not tell about how she promised herself at age five that
she would never be hurt again, and tried to live by that idea for
decades too long.

It did not tell about how she suffered anxiety, worried silly,
arriving at meetings early, fretting over every detail.

It did not tell about how much she wanted control.

It did not tell about how she drove to New Haven when I said
I thought there was something wrong in my head, then took to
her hotel bed.

It did not tell about her oddly charged relationships with my
friends, or with neighbors, how she took people in and dis-
owned them with the same passion.

It did not tell about how she cancelled her subscription to Time
when they published photographs from *Last Tango in Paris*, of
how she resented the condescension of their reply.

It did not tell about how we drove the Pennsylvania Turnpike
in a snowstorm in search of colleges, how the rental car agency
wouldn't rent her the car because she didn't have a job.

It did not tell how she and my father withdrew behind a closed
door to eat peanuts because I am so allergic to them.

It did not tell how she tried to learn to play the piano, Christmas
carols in August, but got no better than first or second year.

It did not tell how she did a needlepoint on her grandmother's
pillow.

It did not tell how her grandmother, Mama, died in her arms in
her late 80s, as she and Martha and her brother Joe laughed over
dinner.

It did not tell how Mama wanted to be a conductor, made large
motions with her arms to the radio.

It did not tell how she said she would never care for a grandchild
of her own, and then how she offered to watch Sangha when we
knew she could not.

It did not tell how her life was woven in with historical time,
how one woman wandered through wars and kitchen appliances
and rights movements and elections.

It did not tell how they named their cars Marfred and Heidi and
TJ.

It did not tell how she and her classmates were allowed to get up
and look out the window when an airplane flew past.

It did not tell how she loved to do crossword puzzles with her
neighbor, Ernie, until he died and her mind escaped.

It did not tell about how angry she was that everyone had
wanted her to act, be artistic, when she should have been an
accountant.

It did not tell how lovingly she kept her books, down to the
penny.

It did not tell how she made monkey faces (yes, it did!), or how
the acting teacher at her college said he had just the part for her
--a monkey on Noah's Ark.

It did not tell of how, as the smallest student in the class, she had
her feet irradiated over and again on the x-ray machine.

It did not tell of how she used to smoke, until she married.

It did not tell of her encounters with Al Jolson or with Marlene
Dietrich. It did not tell how she showed the latter a tent in a field
where she could stay and how Dietrich swept her hand forward
and said, "I vill go on to Rome!"

It did not tell how she could not grieve when her husband died.

It did not tell how she grieved for a Navy officer who killed himself,
because he too was short, "like Fred."

It did not tell how she resented her own family, her husband's
family, but wanted one for her daughter.

It did not tell how she was bitten by a raccoon in her own house,
how she said "it just does you in" of the rabies shot she had to
have, of how it got in the local newspaper.

It did not tell how she asked questions like, "why do you like
Modern Art?" or "do you write only for other poets?"

It did not tell how she'd adored George Bernard Shaw, how she
went to see the Brontë's house and Shelley's "grave."

It did not tell of the set of Shakespeare Mrs. Kidder gave her that
she got rid of when my father died, along with his clothes, his
gold watch, his shoes, her decorative Nazi sword.

It did not tell about the big pieces of pie she cut, or how she
refused to borrow money or take on mortgages in Monopoly.

It did not tell about the wavy brown hair she grew down to her
waist, wrapped up in a bun with bobby pins.

It did not tell about how, when my father died, and the young
doctor entered the room she said, "I trust you're not going to ask
me how I am."

It did not tell how much she loved hotdogs and ice cream sand-
wiches, or how she ate a hamburger in Frankfurt and a frank-
furter in Hamburg.

It did not tell how she sat down one day to write her friends to
say she was not Smokey any more, she was Marty.

--Saturday, June 25, 2011

Acknowledgments & Notes

All the names are real, except those that have been forgotten or misremembered or made-up. Ages are guesses. Names in the poems and the prose are sometimes different, as are the ages assigned to them.

Most sections of this book appeared first, in different form, on Tinfish Editor's Blog (http://tinfisheditor.blogspot.com); sections have been published in *Capitalism, Nature, Socialism* (23:2) 2012; *AlteredScale.com; NAP 2.9; This Corner (Blue).*

The following sections were first published in an e-book, inspired by paintings of old women by Elizabeth Berdann, *Old Women Look Like This* (Liverpool: Argotist Press): "Anne of Manor Care Gables"; "Waiting Adults"; "World Cup"; "Are You My Mother?"; "To An Old Philosopher Dying in a Nursing Home"; "Soap Opera Generator." The e-book is available on-line at http://www.lulu.com/product/ebook/old-women-look-like-this/12287311. Berdann's paintings can be found here: http://www.elizabethberdann.com/gallery_singleHuman.htm.

"World Cup" was choreographed and danced by the Bellingham Repertory Dance Company in collaboration with Chuckanut Sandstone Writers Theater; many thanks to Carla Shafer for making this possible and to Erika Olson for the choreography. I only wish I could have been there to see it.

Many readers & friends are thanked inside the book. I thank them again here for their kindnesses during my mother's long dying. Thank you to Gaye Chan for creating a cover to go with the cover to the first volume.

I want to thank everyone who offered me a place in which to read my work on Alzheimer's over the past few years, including Kaia Sand, Erica Kleinknecht, Leonard Schwartz, Lauren Berlant, John Ernest, Al Filreis, Jaimie Gusman, Carolyn Hadfield, Miriam Fuchs, Laura Lyons, Caroline Sinavaiana, Tony Trigilio and others. I offer my profound thanks to Lissa Wolsak, Joe Harrington, Ben Friedlander, John Emil Vincent, Michael Snediker, Tiare Picard, the many loving caregivers at Arden Courts, Ellen, Steve & Max

Weiss, Brad & Anne Waters, and to all the many people who sent Facebook, email, material notes, & phone calls (Bill Howe!), and above all to Bryant, Sangha & Radhika. You are where I find my home.

Susan M. Schultz is author of several books of poetry and poetic prose, including *Aleatory Allegories* (Salt, 2000), *Memory Cards & Adoption Papers* (Potes & Poets, 2001), *Then Something Happened* (Salt, 2004), *Dementia Blog* (Singing Horse Press, 2008), and *Memory Cards: 2010-2011 Series* (Singing Horse, 2011). *A Poetics of Impasse in Modern and Contemporary American Poetry* was published by the University of Alabama Press in 2005. She edited *The Tribe of John: Ashbery and Contemporary Poetry* (Alabama, 1995) and co-edited, with Annie Finch, *Multiformalisms: A Postmodern Poetics of Form* (Textos, 2009). More recently, EOAGH 8 published a feature she edited on "writing dementia." She edits Tinfish Press out of her home office in Kāne`ohe, Hawai`i and teaches at the University of Hawai`i at Mānoa. She is a lifelong fan of the St. Louis Cardinals baseball team.

Singing Horse Press Titles

Charles Alexander, *Near Or Random Acts.* 2004, $15.00
David Antin, *John Cage Uncaged Is Still Cagey.* 2005, $15.00
Rae Armantrout, *Collected Prose.* 2007, $17.00
Rachel Tzvia Back, *A Messenger Comes.* 2012, $15
Julia Blumenreich, *Meeting Tessie.* 1994, $6.00
Linh Dinh, *Drunkard Boxing.* 1998, $6.00
Norman Fischer, *Success.* 1999, $14.00
Norman Fischer, *I Was Blown Back.* 2005, $15.00
Norman Fischer, *Questions/Places/Voices/Seasons.* 2009, $16
Norman Fischer, *The Strugglers.* 2012, $15
Phillip Foss, *The Ideation.* 2004, $15.00
Phillip Foss, *Imperfect Poverty.* 2006, $15.00
Phillip Foss, *The Valley of Cranes.* 2010, $15.00
Eli Goldblatt, *Without a Trace.* 2001, $12.50
Mary Rising Higgins, *)cliff TIDES((.* 2005, $15.00
Mary Rising Higgins, *)joule TIDES((.* 2007, $15.00
Lindsay Hill, *Contango.* 2006, $14.00
Lindsay Hill, *The Empty Quarter.* 2010, $15.00
Karen Kelley, *Her Angel.* 1992, $7.50
Karen Kelley, *Mysterious Peripheries.* 2006, $15.00
Kevin Killian & Leslie Scalapino, *Stone Marmalade.* 1996, $9.50
Hank Lazer, *The New Spirit.* 2005, $14.00
Hank Lazer, *N18 (Complete).* 2012, $15
McCreary, Chris & Jenn, *The Effacements / a doctrine of
    signatures.* 2002, $12.50
David Miller, *The Waters of Marah.* 2002, $12.50
Andrew Mossin, *The Epochal Body.* 2004, $15.00
Andrew Mossin, *The Veil.* 2008, $15.00
Paul Naylor, *Playing Well With Others.* 2004, $15.00
Gil Ott, *Pact.* 2002, $14.00
Ed Roberson, *The New Wing of the Labyrinth.* 2009, $15
Ted Pearson, *Encryptions.* 2007. $15.00
Susan M. Schultz, *Dementia Blog.* 2008, $15.00
Susan M. Schultz, *Memory Cards.* 2011, $15.00
Heather Thomas, *Practicing Amnesia.* 2000, $12.50
Rosmarie Waldrop, *Split Infinities.* 1998, $14.00
Lewis Warsh, *Touch of the Whip.* 2001, $14.00

These titles are available online at **www.singinghorsepress.com**, or through
Small Press Distribution, at (800) 869-7553 or online at **www.spdbooks.org**